CAPITALISM
FOR
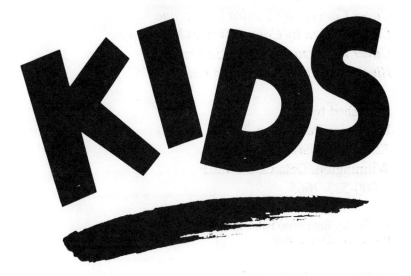

GROWING UP
TO BE
YOUR OWN BOSS

BY KARL HESS

Capitalism For Kids
By Karl Hess
Editorial Research by Randy Langhenry

Cover Concept by Sandra L. Taccone
Cover Design by Connee Wright McKinney
Cover Illustrations by Shokie Bragg
Illustrations by Rozie Zappo Baugh

Published by:
Enterprise Publishing, Inc.
725 North Market Street
Wilmington, Delaware 19801
1-800-533-2665

© 1987 by Enterprise Publishing, Inc.
ISBN: 0-942103-06-8

First Printing, December 1987
Second Printing, April 1990

"This publication is designed to provide accurate and authoritative information in regard to the subject matter covered in it. It is sold with the understanding that the publisher is not engaged in rendering legal, accounting, or other professional service. If legal advice or other expert assistance is required, the services of a competent professional person should be sought."
— From a Declaration of Principles jointly adopted by a Committee of the American Bar Association and a Committee of Publishers and Associations.

Printed in the United States of America

To the Kids

*And to Therese and Marcia
and the Langhenry who is on the way*

CONTENTS

1

MONEY AND YOU

You probably want to make money. There's nothing wrong with that. In fact, there's a lot that is very good about it. It means that you are willing to do things that other people will pay for. It helps you. It helps them.

I hope that you want to do more than just make money. I hope that you want to do things that make you happy, that excite you. I hope that you will never have to do things that bore you or that you hate, just to make money. A lot of people do. One of the reasons you may enjoy starting a business of your own, or getting together with some friends to start one, is that you can choose something that you want to do rather than something you feel you have to do.

Maybe there is something that you want to do that you enjoy so much that you don't even care whether you make money or not. That's wonderful, but remember that someone is going to have to earn the money to take care of you while you do it—unless you can also earn enough on your own to do it.

Even if making money isn't your main goal, remember that money is the way we keep accounts these days. If you don't have any, things will be harder for you than if you have some. Some people don't need much to let them do what they want. Some people need a lot. And it all has to come from someplace. Friends can give it to you. Your parents can give it to you. But someone has to have earned it sometime, someway, someplace.

You can either earn money or you can steal money. You can't just make it appear by magic or by wishing. Sometimes you hear politicians say that they are going to give money to people. Never forget that they have to take it away from some other people first.

Stores sometimes advertise things as being free. They just give these things away. That doesn't mean that they don't cost something. Somebody had to pay for them in the first place. There is no such thing as a free lunch.

And one other thing that I hope you will think about as you begin to read this book and you read every page of it. Some people say they make money by lying to people or cheating them. They certainly can. But actually, when you lie or cheat, you are just stealing. You are not making money by doing honest things that people want. You are lying and cheating. You are stealing. Don't ever be that sort of person. Even if you never go to jail for doing it, lying and cheating will make you a different person, someone who will someday be ashamed to even look in the mirror; someone who other people will eventually know is nothing but a thief (no matter how hard you try to excuse your lying and cheating with fancy names).

The people you may admire most certainly aren't people who accomplished things by lying and cheating, are they?

Above everything else you want to earn one thing that is even more important than money. You want to earn self-esteem. You want to feel good about yourself. You

want to be able to look anyone in the world straight in their eyes and gain their respect. You want to respect yourself.

Money is a way to keep track of how well you're doing. It's just one way. The way you feel about yourself is the bottom line. You should be able to make money and lose money without ever losing your own sense of self-worth and self-respect. Remember, the object is for you to make money by doing useful things, things that other people will voluntarily pay for. You make the money. The money doesn't make you!

2

WHAT KIND OF PERSON ARE YOU?

How do you feel about yourself? What do you think about your place in the world? These are the most important questions you can ask yourself.

Do you believe that you can think for yourself? Or do you have to wait to be told everything?

When you read a book, do you try to understand it on your own? Or do you wait for someone to tell you what it meant?

Do you believe that you are important as an individual? Or do you feel that you are important only as part of some group or another?

When you do something, do you do it because you really enjoy it? Or do you do things because you think that's what other people expect you to do?

Do you believe that when you are older you can work for yourself or with people who get together voluntarily to do something? Or do you think you'll just have to go to work for someone else and do whatever they tell you to do?

Do you believe that people who make and sell things are good and useful? Or do you think that business is bad and greedy and needs politicians to keep it in line?

Do you believe that if you work harder, or smarter, that it's okay to have more as a result? Or do you believe that everybody ought to have an equal share of everything no matter what they do?

Do you believe that you ought to be graded in school on how well you do as an individual? Or do you believe that the entire class should "share" grades and everybody get the same grade no matter what they did?

If most of your friends said that it was okay to steal, would you still say "no it isn't"? Or would you go along with the crowd?

Are there things you have decided are right for you, things that you won't give up just because most people don't agree? Or do you wait to see what most people are doing before you make up your own mind?

Do you enjoy solving puzzles and thinking about things? Or do you always want to have other people entertain you?

Do you think that when you grow older you and your friends can take care of yourselves? Or do you think that only the government can really take care of people?

Do you think that making money is a reward for doing things that other people want? Or do you think that making a profit is bad and greedy?

Do you think that poets and scientists should make money for the things that they do to delight or help people? Or do you think that creative people should "serve" society and not be rewarded for what they do?

Do you think that taking care of yourself first is the only way you'll ever have enough time or wealth to help take care of other people? Or do you think that your first thought should be to sacrifice yourself to the needs of others?

Do you think that a person should do good deeds because he has thought about it and wants to do it? Or do you think that people should be forced to do good things whether they want to or not?

Do you think that people should be free to do what they want as long as they don't prevent other people from doing the same? Or do you think that everybody should live by a single set of rules?

Do you think that people should have their own rules which they agree to with the people around them? Or do you think that a special group of people should make all the rules for everybody?

Do you think that the way to end poverty is to create wealth? Or do you think that the best you can do is to take things from people who have things and give them to people who have less?

Do you think that the best way to make money is to do something that you are good at and that you enjoy? Or do you think that you always have to do things you don't like in order to have a job and make money?

If there was something you wanted to do, something you loved doing, would you try to do it on your own as long as you could and not expect anyone else to pay for it unless they wanted to? Or do you think that just because you want to do something that "society" should support your doing it?

Do you think that you are responsible for the choices you make in life? Or do you think that you are always forced to do things by forces you can't control?

Can you go anywhere and hold your head up because you respect yourself? Or do you feel ashamed of yourself unless other people like you?

If the whole world wanted to go north and you

wanted to go south, would you still try to make the trip? Or are you always trying to follow someone else's roadmap?

Do you think that there are things worth taking a risk for? Or do you think that "society" should make sure that everything in life is absolutely safe?

Do you think that "society," after all, is just a fancy name for other people? Or do you think that "society" has a mystical life of its own and is more important than individuals?

If you answered "yes" to the first question in each of those paragraphs, and if you answered "no" to the second parts, then you are a believer in freedom, the individual, and the free market already. If you answered the questions the other way around, then you are more of a socialist and may not like what this book is all about.

But let's suppose that you are on the "yes" side.

What this book is going to do is to try to encourage you to become active in the free market as soon as you can and at as early an age as possible.

It also is going to try to make the point that people who make and sell things are absolutely necessary in order that the great inventions of science and the tools of technology can enter into our everyday lives and make us healthier and happier.

Let's take an example out of ancient history. The great mathematician Euclid figured out how to prove the ways that you can construct and accurately measure geometric figures. He took an important step toward thinking scientifically so that we could observe the natural world, draw conclusions about it, and use or preserve it for our own purposes.

But suppose there had been no men of business or commerce to understand what Euclid was talking about

and, in turn, use that knowledge for useful and practical purposes? Geometry could have remained nothing but some rules in an ancient manuscript.

Practical men, merchants, adventurers knew that what Euclid had done was to provide a powerful intellectual tool to change and improve everyday life.

Mapmakers had new ways to measure distances. Sailors had new ways to chart their voyages. Neighbors had new ways to measure their land so that one person could be responsible for some while others could be responsible for the next area, and so forth. It gave new dimensions for the meaning of ownership when people could actually measure greater distances than could have been measured just by sticks or ropes. Builders had a new tool for figuring out ways to erect things. It went on and on. It's still going on. Geometry remains one of our great tools, thanks largely to its practical applications by practical people in practical life.

Today, practical people are taking the most advanced ideas of science and technology and putting them to work for people everywhere. Computers have long since moved out of the laboratories and into factories, homes, businesses, entertainment, into every part of our everyday lives.

The people who take the risks involved in getting something new to market, where we can all have a chance to buy and use it, are called entrepreneurs.

They are people who see a need and fill it. They are people who see a possibility where no one else had—and then start a business based on it.

The world was explored in olden times by great navigators sailing on ships provided by entrepreneurs who were willing to risk a lot to find out if there were riches in other parts of the world.

Many great scientists have been backed by entrepreneurs who might not even have understood what the scientist was doing but who did understand that every scientific breakthrough opens up entire new worlds of practical opportunity. Some of history's greatest artists were backed by people who had become rich in commerce and thus were able to support their love of beauty by supporting artists.

Opening new ways to wealth always has moved the life of human beings forward. Although many people on earth still are terribly poor, the gradually increasing wealth of the earth has meant that there are, relatively, fewer of them and that even the poorest can expect help that was never possible before. It has been entrepreneurs who have played a key role in increasing the wealth.

The Bible says that "the love of money is the root of all evil." Perhaps a person who just loved money and didn't care how it was gained could be a very evil person, even a criminal, or a political dictator, or a false prophet. But money just by itself is not an evil. It is a system we have developed to have an easy way to pay for a variety of things rather than just having always to trade things directly. When money, or wealth, is created by doing things that people want to have done or by providing things that people want to own and use, then money is just a measure of how successfully human needs or desires have been met. In that way, you could even say that money can be the root of much that is good.

When you look, these days, at people who are very rich and who earned it all on their own, you are likely to find one thing they have in common. They didn't set out just to make money. It wasn't the money that they loved.

It was some sort of work or activity that they loved. And when they did it very well, and when a lot of people rewarded them for doing it by buying what they were selling, they became rich—and the customers became happier.

That's a great attitude for any young person to have in becoming an entrepreneur.

And now let's look at the various systems that there are in the world today that guide the way people live together and make things.

3

CAPITALISM AND OTHER ISMS

Imagine that you and some of your friends have just found yourselves in a strange new world where there was no one to tell you what to do. The world is full of all the machines that you need to make things. There's plenty of fuel to run the machines. It's springtime. There's plenty of land on which to grow food. There are computers that can give you a way to get all of the information you need to get anything done. And there's enough food in a pantry to keep you going for a while.

What's the first thing that you'd do? Maybe you would want to do nothing; just cool it and hang out for a while. Sorry. That won't work. You're going to have to start planning for food to eat when the pantry goes bare. You're probably going to want some sort of shelter before the winter comes.

You are going to have to make some choices.

Economics, politics, ideology—all of the things you read about in history books, social science books, and in the daily newspapers; all of the things that you see on TV—all of these things are about the way people make choices. And when you think about it, you actually are in a world in which there are all of the things needed to make you happy, to help you do the things you want, and to help everyone else to do the same. And right now you are going to be able to make some choices about how you are going to be part of it all. That's what this book is about: choices, the choices you can make right now to become part of the world of creativity, work, invention, and production. You are never too young to get started.

Every day of your life is filled with choices. Even when you don't think you're making a choice; when you just do what someone tells you—you are actually making the choice to do what someone tells you to do. You could say "no." But you may choose to think that it isn't worth the trouble. That's still a choice.

So here you are in this brand new world that we are imagining and you have to make some choices.

Should everybody learn to run the machines and then rush over and plant some seeds? Should some people work at the computers, while other people work the machines, and some others do the planting? How will you decide who does what? Should everybody do the same thing forever? How will you handle it when somebody wants to do something else? How long will you work? What should you make? How will you divide it up? Who will repair the machines? Who will think about whether you need new ones?

Choices, choices, choices.

Capitalism is one way that people have chosen as a framework or a set of guidelines—a sort of roadmap—for making choices. It is one of many possible sets of guidelines to answer the questions about your brand new world, its machines, its land, the way you'll live together.

The guidelines can be compared to the various other systems of making choices that are available around the world today—systems such as democratic socialism, socialism, communism, and totalitarianism.

Let's start with those other systems and see what sort of guidelines they would have for the new world that you and your friends suddenly are facing.

If you wanted to run your new world according to the guidelines of socialism, a couple of your friends would be elected to make all of the choices for the rest of you. The machines and most of the fuel would be owned, in effect, by those people and so would the land. They would say that it was all owned by the people—but the leaders of the people would control it. They would tell you what you could do and when to do it. Personal possessions, perhaps even some private houses, personal automobiles, and such things would be permitted; but the socialist government would have a powerful voice in saying how they could be used and how much could be owned.

There would be some room for non-governmental business owned and run by individuals. In fact, those private businesses would be counted on to provide the wealth that would pay for the socialist government. But, the leaders of the socialist party in charge would have the last say on everything.

Your new world, then, would look like this: A couple of friends would be elected to be in charge. They would be in charge of all the major machines and most of the fuel to keep them running. They would also be in charge of most of the land. They would decide how many people should work the machines and how many should work the land. They would also decide if you might have businesses of your own, the businesses that would pay the bills for whatever things the socialist government would want to do, such as providing health care for people or paying people to stay home with their children or anything else.

Sweden is a good example of a country that follows the socialist guideline. The government doesn't own all the businesses and factories, but it can tell the people who do own them what to do. Also, the taxes that the government collects from those businesses are used to pay for businesses and services operated by the government. The government-operated businesses don't have to make money on their own.

Great Britain is an example of a country that swings back and forth between the government owning a lot of business and industry and then letting it go back into private hands. It is part way socialist when a certain set of leaders is elected and then part way private enterprise when another set is elected. They are a very mixed economy but with the government having a great deal of control over everything. It also is a country with very great ups and downs in its economy.

There are some countries which call themselves socialist and where the leaders do not want anything but the very smallest businesses to be owned by individuals. They want the government to own all the major businesses and industry. Every one of these countries has had terrible economic problems. Some have tried to solve them by letting more business and industry be operated by individuals instead of government bureaucrats.

Communism would be the guideline that you would follow if a couple of your friends actually kicked the socialists out and took over the whole thing for themselves. Then they would tell you what to do and when to do it. They also would form a political party that would own all of the machines and the land, but they would promise to take care of it so that you would get the best benefit out of it all. You would have the choice of believing them or not, but you wouldn't have any choice about doing what they told you to do. From time to time the leaders might hold elections in which you could vote for the candidates that they selected. Usually there would be only one candidate for each office.

Under communism your new world would look like this: Your friends who would be running the new land would also form a party of the people, and they would let people join it if they promised to obey all of their rules. If you joined you would be better off than people who didn't join. Since the party would own all the machines and all the land, party leaders also would decide who got the food from the land, and how much, and they would decide what should be made on all the machines. They also would decide exactly who should do which job and where they should do it. They might let you have a choice of buying things at the stores they would own—but they wouldn't let you open a store of your own. The standard of living in every single communist country on earth is much lower than the standard of living in countries, like yours, where most of the business and industry is run by individuals who are in business for themselves rather than being government bureaucrats.

A totalitarian guideline for making choices would mean that just one of your friends would take over the entire new world by being stronger than anyone else. It would be someone who could beat up everyone else and anyone who didn't follow orders *would* be beaten up. Everything would be owned by that person. All the rules would be made by that person. Everything you did would be controlled by that person. It would be total power for one leader.

Under totalitarianism your new world would look like this: The Big Boss, the dictator, would get some friends to serve as a personal army or police. If you did anything that the dictator didn't like, the personal army would be sent around to beat you up. If you did everything that the dictator wanted you to, he might even let you have many of the things you want. He really wouldn't care whether you ran the machines or farmed the land. He would only care that someone did it and that they did it exactly as he wanted them to and that they let him have anything he wanted. If you were a close friend of the dictator he might let you have your own business and even let you get rich—but he would always want a bigger share for himself.

All of those systems exist in the world today. To one degree or another they say that the individual ownership of things should either be confined to a few personal items or should be banned altogether. The socialists believe that you should vote for the people who are going to be the bosses but that you should not be able to change the general guidelines. The communists just pick the new bosses as they go along. The communists and the totalitarians have stricter controls on all of their people.

All of the systems have guidelines that work against private property and private profit and the freedom to make and sell what you want, to study and say what you want, or just to be left alone as long as you're not hurting anyone else.

But something very odd started happening in the 1980's. Not a single one of the socialist and communist and totalitarian systems is able to produce enough to keep up with the things that the people in their countries need and want. There is no successful socialist or communist land if you measure success in the freedom of people to make personal choices and to have a lot of material goods and services. Socialist and communist lands are lands where there never seems to be enough for the people and where some people seem to hate the fact they do not have freedom to do things on their own.

The odd thing that is happening, in almost all the socialist and communist parts of the world today, is that the leaders have begun to realize that freedom is important to people, that they work better and harder when they are free, and that trying to plan every little economic detail for an entire country just doesn't work as well as letting people do the planning for themselves.

The things that people all over the world are beginning to turn to in order to try to make their lives better are things that are important parts of—capitalism!

People say a lot of things about capitalism. Some people say that it is very bad. The ones who seem to dislike it the most also seem to misunderstand it the most.

Capitalism is one of the sets of guidelines that people have formed to help them get along better together. It is different from the others we have discussed because of two very important things.

1. Capitalism is based on the ownership of property by individuals, and voluntary associations of individuals. It is a system in which the right to own property is a basic human right. This is the right to own property of all sorts, from land to poems and songs, from little shops to big businesses.

2. Capitalism is based on the freedom of individuals to make any choice they want as long as that

choice does not deny to any other person exactly the same freedom to make choices.

When it comes to making things and selling things,
those two points come together and form what is called the
free market.

A country can be judged as to whether it is capitalist
or socialist or communist by how much it pays attention to
those first two points and then whether it lets people be
free to make and sell things without interference.

No country on earth is completely capitalist today.
And there is no country on earth that permits an absolutely
free market in which people are free to sell or trade things
without any interference at all.

The United States, however, is the most capitalist of
all countries. Free market activities are given as great an
opportunity in the United States as in any other large
nation. And, wherever you look around the world, one
thing seems clear: The more a country lets the free market
operate, the higher its standard of living.

In the United States, ownership of property of all
sorts, from land and poems to music and scientific discoveries, is generally encouraged for individuals. The government, however, demands that taxes be paid on many
forms of property. If the taxes are not paid, the government can take the property. The ownership of property is
not absolute, as it would be in a 100 percent capitalist
country. The ownership of property is conditional upon
paying money to support the government. Also, the
government itself, the federal government plus all of the
state and local governments, actually owns almost 40
percent of all the land in the U.S. And where the government doesn't own the property, it may restrict or control
its use. The United States has what is called a mixed

economy. It is a mixture between mostly free market activities and private property, and government controls and ownership that is similar to that of some of the socialist countries.

One of the very important choices that you will make in your life is whether you want your country to be more capitalist or more socialist.

In a very important way, you and your friends actually will find yourselves in a new world in which you will have to make choice after choice in regard to your own work, the way you live your own life, and the way that rules are set up to make it easier or harder for you to do it in the way that you want.

When you hear people talk about these things, the things they say may sound very complicated. Unfortunately, some people talk about very complicated details rather than discussing the basic facts.

The fundamental fact about the rules that we set up to make it possible for people to live together is that, in the most basic terms, they are all rules that have to do with the relationship between people and property.

First of all, in an absolutely free society, your life and your body are considered the most important private property of all. In an absolutely free society you can say that you do not belong to anyone. You own yourself.

There is no such society on earth today. Even in the most free of all countries, the one in which you live, the ownership of property is not absolute—including the property of your own life and body.

When there is an emergency, the federal government can claim your life and your body by drafting you into the armed forces. Many people agree that this is a good thing for the government to do. They may not trust that enough people will volunteer to help defend the country. But no matter how useful this is, or how necessary some people think it is, the fact remains that this limits your freedom and control of the most personal property of all.

The same thing applies to the activities that you undertake, the work you do, the things you create, your inventions, your discoveries, your poems, your songs— anything you do or make. In an absolutely free society you would own those things and could do whatever you wanted with them as long as you didn't interfere with anyone else's right to do the same with things they own.

One great difference among all systems on earth today is simply how much of what you create you are permitted to keep. In the United States, when the government takes away part of everything you own, it is called taxation. Governments at all levels, from the federal to the local, take tax money from you and spend it for whatever purposes they think are good for people.

Americans vote to choose the people who will decide how much money you can keep and how the rest will be spent. You hardly ever get to vote on the tax or how the government will spend it.

In the United States, when every form of taxation is added up, you will get to keep more than half of what you make and earn. You can do just about anything you want with your half. You can also figure out ways to cut your taxes way down. Some people cut them down to zero. But it takes a lot of hard figuring and usually means that you have to hire a lot of experts to find ways to do it. Most people just pay.

Sometimes, people use tax "loopholes" to keep more of what they earn. It sounds like there's something wrong with it. Some people feel that these loopholes take away money that really should go to the government. Other people say that these loopholes "cost" the government. They say that whatever you keep from the government "costs" the rest of us and is unfair. Also some people believe that these loopholes are just like the government giving money to a select few people.

In some of those criticisms you may get the idea that the government really owns everything and that anything you keep is a special privilege. This is not true.

There is one important thing to keep in mind when you think about government. No matter what else it does that you might like, you need to understand that it does not create any wealth on its own. Everything it does is paid for by money that other people have earned in the market economy.

Whatever the government spends, it first has to get money from the people who earned it.

The only way that government can be said to create any property is when it prints money. It prints a dollar bill for just a few cents that it costs to buy the paper and run the printing press. When it "sells" that new money by putting it into circulation it could be said to have made a huge profit on it.

But, actually it doesn't even make a profit there. All the new money is handled by banks which form the Federal Reserve System. The government's money isn't even called United States money any more. It is called Federal Reserve notes. The amount of new money that is printed every year is decided by these Federal Reserve banks.

Another way that the government "makes" money is by selling bonds to make up for the difference between how much the government spends and how much it receives from all of us in taxes. This difference has been growing greater every year. These bonds can be counted as new wealth because the government sells them to people, to add to the cash it needs at any given moment. Then the government has to pay interest on these bonds. That interest just drives the government deeper in debt and means that more new money has to be printed to keep accounts straight.

Where does the interest money come from? It comes from you and from all people who pay taxes. Right now, the interest on this federal debt takes about one out of every five dollars collected in taxes. It means that millions of people are paying taxes to pay the interest on federal debt and that the relatively few people who buy those bonds get that interest. And, just to make matters more interesting, you don't have to pay taxes on the money you make when you buy government bonds! Buying a lot of those bonds is one way people can keep much more than half of what they earn.

In many other countries you wouldn't get to keep as much of what you earn as in this country. In communist countries whatever you did earn would belong to the people who plan and run the economy. Any time the leaders would want to change the amount you earn, or what you do, or how you spend, they would just issue a new order, and you would have to follow it.

Politics in every country, when you get right down to it, is a substitute for the free market. Politics, rather than voluntary exchanges, is used to decide who gets what— and what gets done.

Everybody seems to have some part of the political system that they like best. Many feel that there are certain things that only the government can do. Political parties usually say that the differences between them involve that sort of thing. One party will say that the government should do most things. The other party will say that it should do fewer things.

But both of the major political parties in the United States agree that in one way or another the government should do a lot of things.

Democrats, by and large, think that the government should regulate business. They don't think that you can fully trust the people who run businesses to regulate themselves, and that if they aren't watched very closely they would make too much money. They do not believe that in the marketplace a seller just gets what a buyer is willing to pay. They think that businessmen sometimes have an unfair advantage, particularly through advertising, and often can make people buy things they don't really want. (Do you think that you spend a lot of money on things you don't want?)

Republicans, by and large, think that government should regulate the way people behave both here and abroad. They do not trust all individuals to behave themselves and think that if they aren't watched closely enough they might say bad things or read bad things or live in ways that are not conventional. Republicans also believe that American soldiers should defend the free world. They think that to defend our country against communism we have to use guns, missiles, and bullets. (Other people think that our ideas of freedom are so much better than the communist idea and that our standard of living is so much higher that we could best compete with and protect against communism by having as much trade with them as possible. When people see how well people live in a market-oriented society, they may want to copy it and not destroy it.)

The reason that a market economy is so productive and that so many people like it is that it lets everyone make choices. Some people make things or offer services. They decide to do those things because they think people want the things or the services. They take a risk. If people do not want the things, then the people who make them can't sell them, and they will be stuck. But the rest of us don't have to share in that loss. The damage that the loss does is limited to the people who took the risk.

On the other hand, if a lot of people decide to buy the things being offered then the business will be successful. The people who took the risk will be rewarded. The people who buy the things will be getting what they want.

In a market system you can make any choice you want. You can decide to make something. You can decide to work for someone else who makes things. You can decide to buy something. You can decide not to buy something. You can hire people to do things for you. You can do things for yourself. You can save your money and go into business for yourself. You can convince other people that what you want to do is good—and you can go into business together.

Because people are always making free choices in a market system, you can quickly know what people want and what people don't want. You can quickly know if prices are too high or prices are too low.

When government tries to figure out those things without letting people make choices in the market, they have to just guess or make up rules without really knowing what people need or want or would be willing to do.

The government tells some people to make things

whether they want to or not. Then they offer those to people whether they want them or not. There is nowhere on earth where that system works very well.

One of the most powerful aspects of a system in which people can own things and make choices is that people who really want to do something, and feel they will be rewarded for it, do much better work than people who are just told what to do whether they want to do it or not.

Even if people are free in most parts of their lives, if they cannot make choices about how and when and where to work it means that they are slaves in their work. Slaves have to do whatever their masters tell them. So do people who cannot make free choices in a free market.

The heart of the market system in which people make choices freely is a process that is called supply and demand.

When the demand for something is very large, people who provide the thing will probably increase their production. They may also raise their prices since so many people want the thing. They have to be very careful, however. If the price goes too high, people will stop buying. Even more important is the fact that as prices rise other people will be encouraged to get into the market. As the price starts to become too high, the other people may just cut their prices. If they do, they'll probably have more customers than the people with the higher prices.

That's an example of price competition. It works to keep prices from going too high.

There is another form of competition, of course. That's the competition that happens when someone makes a product or supplies a service that is simply better than anyone else's. They can charge higher prices and still have a lot of customers because what they sell is known to be so good. When there is this sort of competition, it may make everyone else try to make better things themselves so that they can still attract a share of the customers.

The way that many people get information about things in the market is through advertising. A lot of advertising tries to convince people to buy things just because the ads look so good. And some people buy things carelessly on the basis of the appearance of ads. But they don't have to. Nobody forces anyone to buy anything in a market system. Other people really check out the products they are about to buy. They compare quality. They compare prices. They read reports on the products. They ask people who have used the products what they think about them. So, you can see, advertising is just one way that people get information in a market system.

Just as no one can force you to make any particular choice in the market system, no one can force you to take any particular role in the system. You can choose to work for someone else. You can choose to try and go into business for yourself. You can buy a lot of things. You can choose not to buy anything (if you want to spend the time to grow all your own food, for instance).

The market system is a matter of individual choice in every way.

If you choose to go into business for yourself, no matter how young you are, there are ways to do it. You can start to be a productive part of the market system right now. You can be a capitalist. It's all a matter of choice. It's also a matter of doing good work, and deciding to do that work while a lot of your friends may be choosing to do things that they think are a lot more fun. Maybe you'll decide that working for yourself is the most fun of all.

If you do decide to start working for yourself, you

will very quickly come face to face with the question of private property and of property rights.

Some people do not like attaching great importance to property rights. They say that property should never be more important than people. They are correct. Property never is more important than people. The only reason that property can even be called property is that someone owns it. Property is something that a person or an organization owns.

Property cannot have any rights. It isn't human. Humans, people, have rights. Humans made up the idea of rights in the first place. They have those rights because they agree to them in some way or another or because the people in a powerful institution such as government spells out what their rights are. Rights do not exist by themselves in nature. Rights are something that human beings have thought up.

But, at any rate, the basic rights are all human rights. One human right is the right to own property. Some people say that it is important because unless people own something—a piece of property, an idea, some money, a house, some tools, books, or what-have-you—unless all people can own property they can't plan for their future, they can't make agreements with other people to build things. When only a few people can own property, the few who own it can pretty much tell the others what to do.

In socialist and communist countries, the rulers in the government own so much that they can tell everyone what to do. In communist countries they don't even believe that you own yourself. The government says that it owns you. Communist and socialist governments say that they are against property rights and in favor of the rights of society. But the fact is that they mean they want property to be owned more by the politicians or leaders than by people generally.

In a capitalist society, it is very important that everyone have the right and the opportunity to own property. In an absolutely capitalist society it would be important that the government not try to stop you from owning property. In a mixed economy, such as in the United States, the government has rules and regulations about how much property people can own, and what they can do with it, but by and large the government leaves them alone to own property as they see fit. Once again, you have to remember that throughout your life you are going to have to make choices as to where you stand on this matter. Will you want the ownership of property to be as much a matter of free choice as possible, or will you want the government to step in more and more?

Whenever there are political arguments about property rights, you will hear a lot of talk about human rights being more important than property rights. Always remember when you hear that sort of talk that what it really is about is whether people in general should have the right to own property or whether people in government should make the decisions about owning property. All things that we call property are owned by somebody. The big political debates are about whether you should own some part of it or whether the politicians should own it. When businesses are attacked because someone says they put property rights ahead of human rights, you must remember that businesses are associations of humans—humans who have rights. And one of those rights, a lot of us think, should be the right to own property. The argument is not about property, actually; it is about human rights, which humans should have the right to own property. Should individuals, communities of individuals, companies of human beings, and corporations of human beings own property? Or should the political people own or control property? The issue may never be settled once and for all. But you should think about which direction you want to go. It's never too early to start thinking about that.

There is one other argument about property that you may hear. It says that no one should own any—not the government, not the individual. Property, according to this argument, should belong to everybody. Usually this argument is made about property in the sense of land. It is said that no one should own it, that it should be open to anyone and everyone.

Think about that for a moment. If no one owns it, then no one is responsible for it. How do people take care of property that they don't own? Do they take care of it, or do they just use it?

For instance, suppose that there is some land that everyone has access to. Suppose that it is good for grazing animals. Suppose that you have some animals. You let them graze there. Then someone else brings animals there. Now you might start to worry. Someday, you may realize, all of the grass is going to be eaten. Before that happens you may want to feed as many of your animals as possible. You put more and more animals onto the land that everybody "owns." And then your neighbor does the same. None of you is responsible for the land. Nobody owns the land. It's free. Also, before you know it, the land will be ruined, barren, over-grazed, and not of use to anyone.

If someone had owned the land, they would have been able to take care of it and make sure that it wasn't abused. They would have a motive to do this because it would be their own land, a place where they would want to make a living for years to come. People always take better care of property that they own than of property that they don't own.

Once, in the United States, timber companies cut down vast stands of trees in the Northwestern part of the country. People have come to blame capitalism for this. They say that greedy capitalists cut down all the trees just to make a profit and that they didn't care about planting new trees.

That's very wrong. What happened was that the land was owned by the government. The government wouldn't let individual people or communities of people, or companies, own the land. They would only rent the land to them for a short period. Because the people who rented the land could have no long-term interest in the land, they stripped it as bare as they could during the time that they rented it. Where people have been able to own wooded land, they have taken such good care of it that, today, we have a continuing supply of trees for all purposes.

That's the sort of thing that a free market does very well. It encourages people to plan ahead to make the most of what they own.

No matter how small your part of the free market may be as you get started, it will contribute to the general welfare of people. Some people may call you greedy for wanting to own things and make money. Don't let them get you down. Don't feel guilty about wanting to make money on your own. Don't feel guilty about wanting to do something that you enjoy rather than going along with what your friends want to do. If you'd rather earn money than look at TV, there's no reason for you to feel guilty. You're not hurting anyone. You should be helping people. The way you make money for yourself is by doing something or selling something that someone else wants.

Unless you do that, you simply won't make any money. Is that greedy? It sounds more like a fair trade.

If you are very good at what you do and make enough money to do new things or buy new things to help your business grow, you will be helping all of the people who want to sell things to you. You may even be able to hire people. That will help them. All along the line, the way to make money in a capitalist system is to do things that people want. The more you do for them, the more your income will be. The more jobs there will be. The more you will buy things which will help the people who make those things. This cycle of free market activities goes on and on, and as it does the standard of living of more and more people rises.

Some people think that, if government didn't control capitalists, someday just one capitalist might own everything and have all the money. That's a silly idea. What would the rest of the people do? Of course, they'd just start trading things among themselves and start the creative capitalist cycle all over again. And, come to think of it, who would someone who owned everything be able to sell anything else to? His market would be ended—and yours might be opening!

The free market and private property and the economic action of supply and demand have helped more people to accomplish more things—write more songs, make more inventions, build more bridges, fly farther, heal more people, feed more people, do more of all the wonderful things that human beings want to do—than any other system ever tried on the face of the earth.

Americans are lucky to live in a country as free as

theirs is. Millions of people would like to trade places with them.

The rest of this book is about how you can help to keep the free market alive, and how you can productively be a part of it no matter how young you are.

4

THE
WONDERFUL
WORLD OF WORK

No matter how young you are, you are not too young to work. You can work for yourself, to get money for things you want. You can work to help people in your neighborhood or your town. You can work to help your family. You can work to learn more about something you really love to do. The reason you want to work is up to you. But the fact that you *can* work is one of the good things about living in a country as free as ours.

You've probably heard that there are laws against kids working. There are. Those laws were made when many very young children were being hired at very low wages to work in dark, unhealthy places, doing dangerous and unhealthy jobs, working such long hours that they didn't have any time to learn to do anything different.

Even so, many of those children grew up to start businesses of their own and to be happy with families of their own.

Even today it is very hard to hire children to work and just about impossible to hire them on a full-time basis. But it is not impossible for children to go into business for themselves—to work for themselves, to work with other kids, or to work with their families. They still have to attend some sort of school but when they aren't in school, their time is their own. Some kids go to school right in their own homes. For them, work can just be a part of everyday life.

But why should you work? Some people say that when you are young you should only play. They say that childhood is when you should just act like a child.

How does a child act? Some act pretty silly. Some just want to watch TV. Others just want to play games. Some just want to go shopping.

When Mozart was a child, he wrote great music. When John Paul Jones was a teen-ager he commanded a battleship. When Edison was a kid he was already inventing things. Today there are many kids who are helping make scientific discoveries, who are writing music, who are writing stories, who are painting pictures, who are starting businesses—kids who work.

There simply isn't any one way that kids act. You, no matter how young you are, are a person, a human person with just as much human possibility to do good and even great things as anyone else, old or young.

The idea that kids should only play is an insult to kids. When a young person decides to do something other than play it probably is because that thing they have decided to do is more interesting than playing, more fun.

When you find something you'd rather do than play, you are exactly old enough to stop playing and enjoy something else. Some older people may say that it's a shame you don't act like a child at play as long as you can. They may wish they could just play childhood games again. They may not like the work they do.

Is there something that you enjoy doing more than playing like a child? If so—you should do it! If what you enjoy is called work, you still should do it. If you want to make money doing it, you should try to do it. If you want to do it without making money—and can find a way to do it—that's fine too. The point is that the younger you start doing something that you like to do, something that you can do even as you grow older, the better off you may be. It's never too soon to start.

Why not start today?

Look at what some other young people have done just to get an idea of all the possibilities that there are. Then imagine the ones that you can think of that no one else may have thought of!

Kim Moriarty and Julie Tervo of Lancaster, Massachusetts, started their own business called Country Cats. They began making stuffed pets when they were both 12. They made large-sized cats for doorstops, and small "kittens" for toys and Christmas ornaments. They worked after school and all day during the summer. Julie machine stitched body pieces and Kim embroidered cat faces by hand.

They saved some money they earned and used some of it to buy more materials. Business has been very good. After a while they branched out into calico teddy bears.

Jesse Bartels, age nine, of Laguna Beach, California, made holders for toothbrushes out of clay. The holders were shaped like monsters that he had seen in movies or that he dreams up. His father is a ceramics artist and has a studio near the family's home. Jesse sells his creations at a local craft fair.

Heather Brackeen and Stacey Smit, then both 11, of Albuquerque, New Mexico, opened their own shop called The Weaving Loom. The shop was located in Heather's bedroom. The girls invited friends and relatives to see their shop and to order handwoven scarves, place mats, purses, and pot holders.

The girls began their business when they received looms from their parents for Christmas presents. Their business earned enough money for both saving and spending. The girls also used a home computer to keep track of their expenses and profits.

Nick and Alex Karvounis, twins who were 14, of Timonium, Maryland, juggled and performed magic tricks at children's birthday parties.

The boys saved some of their profits for college and used some to buy new magic equipment.

Three girls, at ages 10, 11, and 12, ran their own business in Bexley, Ohio. The girls started Mini Recyclers. They went through the neighborhood trash cans to find items that needed minor repairs, painting, sewing, cleaning, or mending. The girls sold their wares through a thrift shop that is run by the Cancer Society, and profits were split between the girls and the Society.

Michael Whiting, of Douglas, Alaska, started being a commercial fisherman when he was eight. His brother Cory was also a fisherman by the age of 11. Michael mainly worked on his father's boat, but he also worked for other fishermen. Michael set out nets, cleaned fish, put the catch on ice, and did other jobs. He worked full-time during the summer. "You have to learn to get by on little sleep, and you can't be afraid of blood, dirt, or heavy loads," Michael said.

Hal Abrams, of Denver, Colorado, was 14 when he made his own three-minute movie and sold it to a national TV show. The movie took him only a few weeks to make. The film was about a prairie dog town near his home.

Javier Corral Jurado, at only 13, of Ciudad Juarez,

Mexico, was the founder, reporter, photographer, editor, ad salesman, and publisher of *El Chisme*, "The Gossip." His newspaper was published every two weeks for 1,500 readers.

The sixth grade class at Buckingham (Pennsylvania) Elementary School formed their own company as part of a class project to learn more about business. The kids decided to print and sell T-shirts. They sold the shirts to businesses through the mail. The money they earned went to charity, to buy books for the school, and to pay for class trips.

Donny Kanz, then seven, of Hendricks, Minnesota, decided to be a welder. He made and sold hammers by cutting pieces of metal with an electric saw, welding pieces together, and then grinding the rough edges. Then he painted the finished product. It took him about 15 minutes to make each hammer. He sold the hammers to truck drivers for their repair kits. Donny works in his father's welding shop.

When Carson Levit, of Belvedere, California, was 14, he saved $1,000 from a newspaper route. He became interested in the stock market after reading a book about investing in stocks. He invested his $1,000, and 14 months later his investments were worth $8,000. "Investing takes a lot of hard work. I research all my companies," he said. When he gets older he said that he hopes to be a basketball player and an investment banker.

Shawn Welcome, at 13, of Sedro Woolley, Washington, worked in the summer as a logger. He hooked cables around downed trees and a machine pulled the trees off the mountain. He often began work at 3 a.m. He wants to be a full-time logger when he finishes school.

Here's a report on young people who go into busi-

ness for themselves from one of the country's most respected magazines, *Nation's Business,* November, 1985:

"At 15, Robert Lewis Dean borrowed $1,500 from
his parents, bought a 1972 Cadillac and fixed it up, then
sold it for a profit. That was the beginning of his career that
has included starting a business at 16, selling it for
$100,000, and starting other businesses. Still a teenager
(then), Dean operated a variety of businesses dealing with
limousines.

"Surveys have shown that more than half of all
entrepreneurs are first born children, and many are from
immigrant families. Some are mainly motivated by
money, but most are driven by desire to shape their own
destinies.

"Certainly all possess qualities that one might expect in such an individual: ingenuity, a good intellect, a
healthy sense of self, inner drive, and a sense of purpose.

"Perhaps the most engaging quality of teenage
entres is effervescent optimism. Reared in an era of
terrorism, disaster and threat of nuclear mayhem, they
have developed into positive-thinking achievers.

"They fell in love with the business world early and
quickly evolved beyond the normal childish money-
making ventures of selling lemonade, babysitting, etc., to
become bona fide business persons. They are a product of
a generation raised to appreciate the art and science of
business.

"Verne C. Harnish, national director of the Association of Collegiate Entrepreneurs, says, 'The young entrepreneur is emerging as this generation's hero. There's
beginning to be a movement to introduce entrepreneurship on the high school, junior high school and even
elementary school level. Society is going through a

transition. We're entering an information age.'

"A teenage business often begins modestly but builds with speed. John Shorb started mowing lawns for hire when he was in the sixth grade. He concentrated on building a clientele in the affluent neighborhoods of upper northwest DC. By the time he entered high school, he knew how to care for every type of outdoor plant that grows in the DC area. Today at 19, he is president of Northwest Lawn Service. His gross sales will approach $125,000. Within 10 years he plans to be operating the major horticultural center in DC.

"Young entrepreneurs 'have seen the future — and it is theirs.'"

One of our favorite stories is about a kid who went into business for himself. The information is from the magazine *Black Enterprise*, June, 1986. Kenneth Carter is 15 years old and has been the owner, operator, and CEO of TC Catering Service in Gary, Indiana, since he was 13. His father is a steelworker, and his mother is a police officer. He has four brothers and doting grandparents who have always supported his entrepreneurial ventures. He has been working most of his life, selling everything from newspapers and hot dogs to candy and Christmas cards.

"I got into business early because I couldn't find anyone who would hire me to work for them," Carter says.

He is an articulate and poised young man; he favors business suits and ties and always carries a briefcase whenever he makes public appearances. He is on the mayor's youth advisory council, has been on "Donahue," and has toured the country as a youth representative for the National Baptist Convention.

At the age of 12, Carter attended a wedding reception that was catered. Spotting his opportunity to gain some hands-on experience, he approached the owner and offered his services as a volunteer in the kitchen. After he showed he could more than do his work, the owner offered him a salary.

Then he thought he could offer the same services for less cost. He talked about the idea of starting his own catering business with friends, mostly high school seniors and college freshmen, but they tried to discourage him.

"They didn't think I could do it. Of course, their doubts only made me more determined," he said.

After working for the other caterer for six months, he left to open his own business.

"Some people still see me as a child. Even though I'm fifteen years old, I will not be walked over. So I have to tell them politely that I know my business."

Carter's permanent staff of 10 includes an assistant manager and a driver who owns the van they use (Carter is too young to have a driver's license). Both of these men are 18 years old. The other eight males and females are all schoolmates of Carter's, and are between 14 and 16 years old. They work as waiters or dishwashers.

He has learned the advantage of taking care of his own money. Soon after he started TC Catering Service, he opened a bank account in a neighborhood bank. Later when he wanted to withdraw some of the money, he was told by the bank that he could not do so without a parent's signature. His mother was at work, so Carter stood his ground replying "If I was old enough to deposit the money, I'm old enough to take it out." And he did—all of it.

Recently he grossed about $10,000.

The traditional symbol of a job for a kid is the summertime lemonade stand on the sidewalk of a suburban home. There's nothing wrong with that. The more

lemonade stands the better.

But let's take a close look at the lemonade stand and try to understand how it can be less than a real business— something that would teach a bad lesson rather than a good one for a kid who wants to start a business.

A parent may have bought all of the lemons used for the lemonade. The kid running the stand might just take that for granted and not think that for the stand to really make money it would have to make enough to pay back mom or dad for all the lemons—as well as have some left over. The left over part would be called profit. It would be the money you actually earned by operating the lemonade stand.

But there are other things you have to consider. If you don't consider them you aren't running a business, you are just playing at running a business.

Suppose that the pitchers you use to mix and serve the lemonade are from the family cupboard. If you were running a real business those pitchers would be part of what is called your capital equipment, the equipment that is absolutely needed before you can even get the business started. The lemons would be part of your raw materials.

The point is that you have to get your capital equipment from someplace. It usually won't be given to you. One way to get that capital equipment would be to offer stock, or shares, in your company. Those shares are what you trade to somebody if they will give you the money to buy your capital equipment.

So let's get back to the pitchers for your lemonade stand. To make the stand a real business you might sell your parents a share of your business for letting you have the pitchers. That would mean that they would share in any profits that you made. Since they might also put up the money for the lemons, they might get another share for that.

Now what about the space on the lawn that you are going to use? In a real business you would either have to buy or rent the space for your business. So, to make your lemonade stand a real business, you should decide how much rent you'll pay for the space.

Then there's the ice. It isn't free. Someone had to pay for the electricity used to make it. In a real business that cost would be very important and you would have to know how much it amounts to right down to a fraction of a penny.

And don't forget the cost of the cups you'll use to serve the lemonade. And what about the cost of the signs that you put up to tell people about your lemonade stand? That's advertising. You should know what that costs also, right down to the penny.

Why is it important to know all of this? Why, if you *didn't* know it you would have absolutely no way of knowing whether your business was successful or not. You wouldn't have any way of knowing how much to charge for the lemonade. You wouldn't even know if you should start the business in the first place.

No matter what sort of business you might decide to start, you will have to know everything about the costs involved. Don't leave anything out. The difference between success and failure may be just the few cents you forget to account for.

For instance, in talking about the lemonade stand we didn't put anything aside for sugar. Certainly some of your customers would want the lemonade sweeter than others. Having a choice of sweet or tart lemonade might be an important selling point. But you have to figure in the cost of the sugar.

And suppose you get one of your friends to help you run the lemonade stand. You could hire your friend. That would mean that you would promise to pay a certain amount of money (wages or salary) to the person for helping you. You would have to pay that money whether the stand did any business or not. That's the cost of labor. It's a fixed cost if you agree to pay it no matter how much business you do. One way you could change that would be to make the person a partner. That would mean that they would share in whatever money the business did make—after paying all of the cost of production!—but they would also share in whatever losses there might be if the business didn't do well.

What about paying yourself? Well, to be realistic about it, because the business is really yours, you are going to have to pay yourself out of whatever is left over after everything else is paid. That money is called profit and one of the great advantages of having your own business is that you can decide exactly what to do with that profit. You could keep it all. You could put some in the bank. You could use it to buy more lemons and cups and things. You could use it to start another business. You could spend it all on a record player—on anything you want. Because you took all the risk, because you were the entrepreneur, you can claim the reward. But don't forget, it all *is* a risk. If everything went wrong and you didn't make any money at all, you could end up owing a lot instead of making a lot.

Taking risks is the heart of success in the free market. People who take risks make jobs for other people. They can hire people who don't want to take risks. They provide goods and services that people want. They make life a little better for a lot of people. They can get very rich. They can go stone broke. The fact that they aren't afraid to take the risks is why they are so important to all of us. And when you decide to start your own business—no matter how small it is and no matter how small or young you are, you become one of those very useful people; you become what is called an entrepreneur, a risk taker, a creator, a productive human being.

For a venture into work or business to be important for you as a kid, it has to be a venture into the real world in every sense. For it to be an important part of your future it should inspire a *spirit* of enterprise as well as an experience of enterprise.

You don't want to just go through the motions of cute, little jobs that your parents might like to brag about to their friends. You want to do something which is useful and real and would be important if an older person did it and not just because a kid is doing it. You want to be a real entrepreneur, not a playtime cartoon of a little business-man.

You may be familiar with a television character called Alex Keaton, on the show "Family Ties." A lot of people said that he was a model of a young businessman. A lot of people thought that he was funny. The fact is that the character of Alex Keaton wasn't that of a businessman or an entrepreneur at all. He just talked a lot about business. But he didn't actually have a business. He didn't actually work.

Talking about capitalism and being an entrepreneur is easy. It may make people think that whoever is doing the talking is very serious. But there's an old saying that goes "talk is cheap." What really counts is action.

And *just* working isn't the important thing about

gaining the sort of risk-taking, creative spirit that is the most exciting part of capitalism and the free market.

You could, for instance, go and get a job at a fast food place after school. Or you could mow the neighbor's lawn. Or you could babysit for a few people. That would be doing work, all right. It is not working, however, that makes an entrepreneur. Starting your own business involves risk-taking and planning ahead as well as work.

Don't get this point wrong, however. The kid who takes a job like those mentioned in order to save up money to start something different is raising capital. The kid who takes such a job in order to buy fancy clothes or something like that is making a choice also. They may not want to start a business. They may not be thinking about working toward their future at all. The kid who takes such a job because the family needs the money is doing something that has to be done no matter what else. Even such a kid might want to think seriously about a time when they could do a whole lot better by going into business for themselves, or learning skills that will help them be in a position to have more choices.

Let's take babysitting as an example of what we're talking about.

First there is being a babysitter. Even that simple chore can involve economic and market analysis that a kid can make. But beyond that there is babysitting as a potentially expanded market opportunity: A kid might be able to set up a babysitting coordinating service, establish standards, train the sitters in the group, provide a back-up emergency call service, and become an employer of other beginning babysitters rather than just doing the sitting.

Just hanging around the grocery store waiting for people who need help carrying bags may be out of fashion and not even in demand. But any kid who lives near a senior citizen housing unit might want to make a market survey of what the folks there need. A market survey would require you going out and simply asking people if they would be interested in your service, and what they might be willing to pay you to provide the service.

Your service could include some shopping chores. It could include help in moving things, in redecorating. It could include home perms. And a kid entrepreneur could organize other kids to provide some of it as well as just doing a chore alone.

One kid and a lawnmower or one kid and a snow shovel can do a certain amount of useful work on a hot or cold day. One kid scouting neighborhoods for customers, and with some other kids ready to do the work, is a corporate manager already.

Kids might want to sell Christmas trees. Look at the alternatives.

They might agree to help out some established seller of trees. They might, in short, get jobs. They can be sure that the jobs won't pay high wages. They aren't, after all, worth high wages.

They might talk it over with their folks and canvass the countryside looking for someone who would supply trees at a reasonable cost which they could, in turn, sell for a profit undoubtedly greater than the wages of working for someone else.

It would be riskier, of course.

They might choose a location where no customer ever would show up. They might get caught in a price war in which the prices of trees offered by others would fall below the price they paid to buy theirs. Even so, they would learn as much about business in that relatively painless way as they might after spending thousands of dollars for a business course later on.

They might talk it over with their parents and work out the investment possibility of taking some of the money put aside in the family for their future education and investing it in some rural land on which they'd plant Christmas trees for sale in 10 years—perhaps at just the time the education money would be needed. Not only are there valuable lessons to be learned here in the long-term dedication to an agricultural project, but also there are lessons that would be learned in economic analysis, purpose, and long-range planning.

Suppose you decided to wash cars in your neighborhood. A lot of kids have tried that as a way to make money. And it usually works. But let's take the washing of cars a few steps farther—thinking about it the way an entrepreneur might.

First, you want a competitive edge. You want a reason for people to hire you to wash their cars rather than someone else. One reason might be that you could appear to be better prepared. You could have your own sponges, your own chamois cloth for wiping the car dry. You want anything that will show that you are just a bit more serious about washing cars than someone who just shows up and says they want to wash cars but will have to use all of the customer's equipment.

Then you might want to think about merchandising and advertising. You could write up a letter-size poster announcing your car washing service. A local printer could give you a couple of hundred copies for a fairly low price (part of your investment in your own business), or you could ask the printer if he would print the posters in exchange for your washing his car or the company cars enough times to make up for the cost of printing.

Your ad should make clear what services you can offer. Can you wax cars? How much? Do you clean out the inside of the car as a regular part of your service? Will you wash cars at the customer's convenience or will you have a regular schedule of when you can wash cars? Any extra touch you can think of will help your effort and make your car washing stand out above someone else's.

Then, as an entrepreneur, you might start thinking about variations on your car washing business. How would it work if you hired a few other kids to actually do the washing while you concentrated on meeting customers and getting their orders? Could you generate enough business to pay those other kids plus have something left over (a profit) for you and also some money to buy new supplies or to try new advertising?

And what about customers that other kids might not have thought about? Used car lots, for instance, like to keep their cars clean, inside and out. When they take a car in, it may be pretty dirty. Someone has to clean it up. It might make more sense for the car dealer to hire you— particularly if you could prove that you would do a first-class job, than to do it himself or to hire someone full-time to do it.

One kid, in Wichita, Kansas, started out washing cars, then went on to washing big 18-wheel trucks. He's still in high school, but he has so many customers for washing the big trucks that he has hired a bunch of grown-ups to do the work while he gets new customers and manages the entire operation, getting supplies, making sure people do a good job.

Remember, when you are looking for new customers, it never hurts to ask. All the person can do is say no—

and even if they do say no they will at least know that you are a kid who is willing to work and who has some imagination about it. That's a good reputation to get and may prove to be worth a lot in your future years. It's another investment, an investment in reputation.

In every kind of work that you think of, the suggestions made about babysitting, Christmas trees, and car washing can be useful.

Think of reasons why you are a better choice for doing the work than someone else.

Think of additional services that make your offer stand out.

Think of things that will let people know that you are serious and that you can perform good work, that you are skilled and honest, and do your work on time.

Think of whether you could do better if you hired some other kids.

Think of whether you could do better by getting customers and hiring others to do the work.

Think of every single place where you might find customers, and never be satisfied just with the obvious places.

Think. That's your most valuable asset as an entrepreneur—and as a human being!

5

YOUR
FRIEND
THE COMPUTER

Your mind is your most important resource, asset, and tool. It is more important than money. You could have tons of money, and if you didn't use your mind well, you could lose all your money very quickly. You could have acres and acres of land or a big factory, and if you didn't use your mind well, you could lose it all. You could be very strong, but if you didn't use your mind well, about all you could do with your strength would be to dig ditches or lift heavy things for someone else.

In the past, most physical tools, metal tools, wooden tools, or other tools were just extensions of your body. They helped you do things that you couldn't do with your strength alone.

But in your lifetime there is a new tool that isn't an extension of your body but is, instead, a true extension of your mind. That tool is the computer.

You probably know some kids who think that a computer is just a gadget for playing games. The games are great, no doubt about that. But if you use a computer just to play games you are wasting one of the most marvelous inventions in human history.

The best thing about a computer is that you can learn

important things just by understanding how to use it.

You will learn that actions have consequences. You will learn that when you do something, it causes other things to happen. Working with a computer, every instruction that you give the machine results in something happening. And who is responsible for it all? Is the machine responsible? No. It doesn't really know anything. It can only do what you tell it to do and what it is programmed to do.

When you learn how to use a computer, and particularly when you learn to program one, you will learn to be very careful. The computer doesn't tolerate mistakes. You have to be absolutely responsible for making sure that everything is correct. You are responsible. That's an important lesson to learn about life in general.

You will also learn how to break problems or projects down into understandable steps. No matter how big a problem or a project is, it actually is composed of many smaller parts. The more you understand the parts, the better you'll understand the whole thing. When you work with a computer you will go step by step, building as you go along.

You will learn how to see things as a flow of small steps or separate parts. A lot of people just throw up their hands when they see something complicated. They say it's too much for them, and they let someone else worry about it. Working with a computer will help you avoid that helpless feeling. Step by step, as you build your ability to create a program for your computer, you will be using your mind in a logical way that should help you understand many, many other things.

Some people say that computers can never help you understand important personal things, like music or poems, or being in love. But maybe even in those areas, working with the computer will help you feel that you can at least think about even personal problems in a step-by-step way. This hardly means that those flashes of understanding which we call intuition are not important. Far from it. Even when you are programming a computer or using it to keep track of things or whatever—even then you will have many times when a sudden flash in your mind, a flash of intuition, will seem to do more to solve something than hours of hard thinking. That's one thing that computers don't have so far: intuition.

Also, you may discover that your computer actually can help you compose drawings and even music. You and your computer face an unlimited world of creative opportunity together. The computer as a word processor should help you with a skill that many young people seem to be losing. That skill is writing clear and simple sentences. Very often this skill is the major difference between success and failure of a project or a plan. It might even be the most important difference in how you get ahead in life and what you are able to do. The younger you are, the more important this is. Because you are young, a lot of older people will have trouble taking you seriously anyway. If you can't let them know very clearly what you want to do, or what help you might need, you aren't going to get very far. Just standing there and mumbling isn't going to impress anybody.

When you write something on a computer, even if it's just a note to yourself to get your thoughts straight, you can easily change things over and over again without any trouble of the sort you'd have if you were writing with a pencil or even a typewriter. You can keep changing things until they are absolutely clear. Clear thinking is absolutely important.

But remember. The computer is just a tool. The most important part of it all is the person using the tool, the mind of the person using the tool.

There is a problem you could have—unless your parents already use and like computers themselves. Some older people get all of their information about computers from TV shows and movies that show computers as mysterious devices often with minds of their own. They may think that just having a computer in the home is going to solve a lot of problems. Sometimes, when older people think like that they are very disappointed when they actually get a computer. They soon learn that the computer is just an extraordinary machine, but that human beings still have to do the thinking that makes them so valuable. Sometimes this will discourage them and they may build up a real dislike of computers. If your parents have had an experience like that, you need to be patient with them, explain computers as best you can to them, and help them to understand that the computer is a powerful tool and that you have real and good reasons for having one.

Almost the reverse of that sort of problem could happen if there is a computer in your house that is used mainly for playing games. You may need to make a strong case for a separate computer for your own business plans. Also, when you look around for software for your computer, at the ready-made programs that can help you set up a data base to keep track of things or an accounting system to keep track of your costs and profit, be sure that you check out the many magazines devoted to rating such things. Then talk to people in computer stores or in other businesses. One thing for sure, don't buy your software on

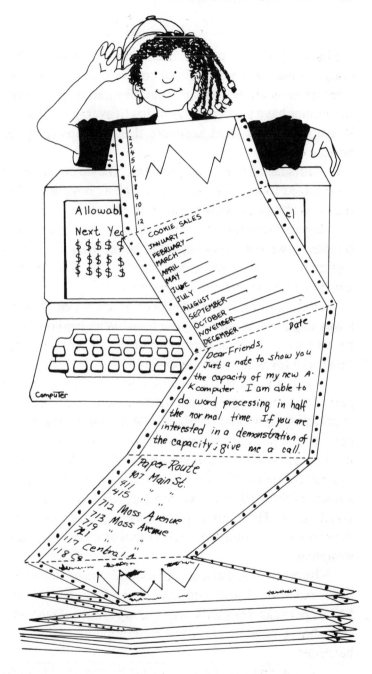

the basis of what you have been using in school. This doesn't mean that your school software isn't good, but some schools are limited in what they can buy and they sometimes have to get programs that fit average demands. If available, you want software that will answer your needs exactly.

Girls face a particular problem. They usually aren't encouraged to use computers as much as boys are. One reason is that many kids begin their interest in computers by playing computer games. Many of the games are oriented toward a direct appeal to boys. This just means that girls have to be more persistent if they want to take advantage of this marvelous machine.

But, boy or girl, the main point is to consider finding a way to get a computer of your own. Whether you use it for an entrepreneurial enterprise or not, it will be a true mind-tool for whatever interests you.

You should think seriously about devoting some part of your earnings, from whatever work you can do, to purchasing your own computer. What kind should you get? You'll just have to make up your own mind on that. But it is fairly safe to say that there really isn't such a thing as a bad computer. Some are slow, some are limited in the amount of things they can remember, but they all can help you do a lot. They can help you do things that you might never do without one. And all of them will help you think straighter.

Recently, the outstanding monthly magazine *Family Computing* (730 Broadway, New York, NY 10003, $19.97 per year) selected a "computing family of the year" that shows how the family that computes together is benefited.

The winners of the award were Bernard and Glenda

Ofstehage and their children Steven, Daniel, James, Peter, and Andrew. They live on a farm in Elk Point, South Dakota. The mother wrote in to enter the contest and tell why they should be the computing family of the year.

Kids use the computer with all kinds of educational software, math, spelling, and reading. Son James is in the first grade now, and has "probably benefited from the computer more than any of us," according to Mom.

During the past year, James suffered a hearing loss, so Mom made up games and activities on the computer to teach him colors, numbers, letters, and reading. This helped him keep up with his kindergarten classmates. His hearing is fine now, but he gained confidence by using the computer. (The benefits of computers to handicapped kids should be obvious.)

Dad uses the computer to keep financial records for the farm. "The spreadsheet makes it easy to show projections and the year-to-year operation of the farm," he said.

Mom uses the computer to keep up with her broiler chicken and egg business.

"The children's awareness of the wealth of learning that the world has to offer is so easily awakened by their computer experiences. It's really fun watching them learn. We are a family that likes to spend a great deal of time doing things together, and our computer has been a superb investment. We can share our recreational and learning time with our computer, as well as use it individually in our work, play, and school activities," Glenda said.

The computer can help you with many projects you undertake. But the computer also can be a project in itself, a tool for a business based on the computer itself.

Here are some examples of what other kids have done with their computers.

One youngster offered to bring his portable computer to birthday parties in the neighborhood. For a $25 fee, he offered to provide printed souvenirs of the party, with each child's name on his or her own souvenir. Also, he programmed his computer to give "Simon Says" and other game instructions. For a bonus, that most kids liked best of all, he let the birthday party-goers type out their own messages on the keyboard and then printed them out.

Here's what a 12-year-old girl in California had to say about her experience with a computer. "Computers have changed my life by letting me get extra credit in school and extra money at home. At school, I typed reports and helped a class of kindergarten children learn how to use a computer. I played lots of educational games with them. At home, I have typed and designed graphics for relatives and friends. I have taught my Mom and brother how to use our computer. I have even created some games of my own."

When Adam Marsh and Stephen Mumford were 15, they created "The Illustrated SAT," a humorous yet effective program and booklet that teaches vocabulary from the Scholastic Aptitude Test. Marsh wrote the BASIC program, and Mumford created the illustrated booklet using an Apple IIe and a mouse. Their program won second place in the Apple Computer Club Competition.

But the two boys wanted more, so they decided to start a company to sell their program commercially. They went to the bank and secured a $15,000 line of credit, got a lawyer and an accountant, and formed Marsh and Mumford, based in Berlin, Maryland. They also claim to be the "youngest people to get Choice, Visa, and Master-Card credit lines in the state of Maryland."

Since then, they have developed a comic book to

discourage hackers from pirating software, and it won first place in the Apple Computer Club Competition.

An even more typical story concerns a 17-year-old kid who is creating and selling his own software in his hometown of Muncie, Indiana. He has an Apple computer and is interested in "machine language bit-mapped graphics and new ways to create sound on the Apple's limited speaker."

He started by writing a simple program for his mother, who is a first-grade teacher. It turned out to be too complex for students, but the teachers liked it and praised his work. So he added two more tutorials and created what he calls "The Science Pack."

The pack includes programs about tooth care and structure, planets and the solar system, and simple plant structure. The school's computer manager suggested he take the program to a teaching supply store in town. They suggested some changes and made some corrections.

"We then determined how it would be sold, the price, what percentage of profit the store would receive, and how the sales manager would contact me — quite a lesson in business!" the young entrepreneur said.

"So, as you can see, I'm not a software star. But I am a 16-year-old with quite a bit of extra spending money and a great deal more programming skill than I started with!"

A kid who definitely is a software star is Jeff Gould, who, when he was 17, already owned his own company, Double-Gold Software, Inc. Double-Gold markets his computer security system called Lock-It-Up. At 17, his work was grossing $100,000 a year, and he had his own suite of offices in California's famed Silicon Valley. He got started on computers when he was 13, and two years later he dropped out of high school to work on them full-time. His first success was a program that taught people how to solve the famous Rubic's Cube puzzle. Now he's gone back to school, taking college courses in finance, while he continues to operate his business.

An even younger computer entrepreneur is Rawson Stovall, of Abilene, Texas, who, when he was 11, started writing a weekly video game column called "The Vid Kid," which has been published by 27 newspapers. He has also written a book on computer games.

Commenting, in a joking fashion, on the ease with which so many very young people turn to high tech work, an article by Andrew Feinberg in the *New York Times* says that "It seems that youngsters are finally learning what adults have always known: that lemonade stands are not on the cutting edge of the economy...

"...in some fundamental way children were supposed to be entrepreneurs all along. It's clear that they possess all the requisite traits. They are energetic, obsessive, stubborn, temperamental and impossible—perfect little creatures of commerce."

Having looked at some real-life examples of ways in which kids and computers have worked together, let's review the machine itself, looking at the ways it can help a business of any sort.

Whenever you want to make a written presentation to someone, telling them what you can do, or when you want to print a handbill telling about your service, or for any purpose that needs something written out, your computer and a printer can do a neat, professional-looking job. Most computers these days also can handle programs that have graphics on them, pictures and designs, that can make your presentation stand out.

If you get good at using those sorts of programs you

might find some business right in your own neighborhood or town by designing handbills for businesses, ads for yard sales, or notices for local clubs.

We've already discussed what a good word processing program can do to help you print out perfect letters or forms or whatever you or someone else wants. Even if you are not a good typist, you can still turn out perfect documents by being very careful and redoing your work wherever you find an error—and unlike typing, correcting the errors won't be any trouble at all. Then, when it's perfect, you can just print out the document.

Many word processing programs also include a mail-merge feature which lets you compose a single letter and then address it, as though each one was done personally, to hundreds or thousands of people. Some small business that doesn't have its own computer might be interested in having you do occasional mailings for them. Also, if you learn how to use this mail-merge feature really well and also learn how to keep names and addresses accurately on file, you probably could make a lot of friends, and maybe find some future customers, by offering to do the mailings and keep the lists for a local charity or church or volunteer group.

If you can afford it, you might buy a modem for your computer—the device that permits you to contact other computers over the regular telephone lines. There are some relatively inexpensive services such as Compu-Serve which will let you use your modem to tap into huge national data banks which keep huge files of everything from newspaper stories to magazine articles and information from every sort of technical publication. There are extra charges for using those big data bases, but it does mean that no matter where you live, you have the potential to get all the information you could possibly need about anything that you could possibly be interested in.

If you want to keep your own financial books, or your family accounts, with the same sort of systems that professional accountants use, you will have to look into what are called spreadsheets. Your local computer store can brief you on them. As with the other features of your computer, if you get very good at understanding and using a spreadsheet, you might find some organization that will pay you to do it for them—or, again, you might volunteer your services to do it for a local volunteer group and, thus, make an investment in your own long-range reputation in the town.

One of the things that a computer can help you do best of all is to manage a lot of information—everything from real data about how to do things, to the names and addresses of potential customers. Because of the many ways that computers can help you easily cross-reference even the most complex sorts of information, you might say that computers are the ultimate filing system. If you handle a data base management program correctly, you will never be at a loss for where you saw something or where you put it. And, of course, the better you are at it and the younger you start, the better your chances of making it a useful part of your long-range plans and dreams.

6

THE FAMILY THAT WORKS TOGETHER

Did you ever dream that you could stay home and do everything that you wanted? You could learn everything you want without having to go to school. You could have good times all day long with your entire family. You could make money. And you could still have time left over to take trips or do other things away from home. Could such a dream come true?

Well, it already has for hundreds of thousands of people who do all of their work at home and even teach their children at home. We'll talk about going to school at home later in this book. Right now, we'll concentrate on the possibilities of an entire family working together at home.

Actually there was a time in America when even more people did just what we're talking about. In the days when there were at least 10 times as many farms in America as there are now, entire families worked together to run their family farms. The work was very hard and although many outstanding people grew up that way, the young people on such farms didn't have much time to do anything but work and work.

Things are certainly different today. People who work at home are using different tools and techniques, and they have many more opportunities than the people who worked on farms that used to take almost every hour of every day to keep going.

A family farm today could be a lot different from a family farm of yesterday. In Maryland, Walter and Sylvia Ehrhardt operate a very modern and profitable farm that grows berries and fine vegetables for big city restaurants. Rather than using high-cost chemical fertilizers, the Ehrhardts use only fertilizers found naturally. The secret of their success is a very scientifically accurate knowledge of the soil and the needs of each thing that they grow. Until their children grew up and went off for careers of their own, they all worked together on the farm. Sometimes the work was hard and long, but there was always time for family outings and for other family activities right there on the farm.

Not far from that farm there is a home industry that makes cotton clothing which is sold all over the world by mail order. The industry was started by two families who wanted a place where their children could be with them all day long—learning regular school subjects as well as learning all the things you need to know to make a productive enterprise work well. Their business, which they call Deva, sells a million dollars worth of clothing each year but, still, all of the people working there take time off every day to play volleyball or other games together. And there usually is opportunity for neighborly talk or even philosophical discussions and, in every way possible, the children of everyone who works there are encouraged to be part of the activity.

As with many other home businesses, Deva didn't

start with a business plan but with a personal plan. The people who started it set as their first goal doing work which could be done in a home setting, and which would keep their families together. They looked carefully at many businesses and saved as much as they could for start-up capital.

They decided on clothing because much of the work, the actual sewing, could be done by other people, in their own homes. The people who started it could concentrate on researching the market—finding out what kind of clothing there was demand for but not much supply. They could also concentrate on how to market the clothes. Natural cotton, loose fitting, super comfortable clothes filled the bill.

The elements of starting a home business are just about the same for anyone who wants to think about it.

First of all, you have to be very clear about risk. If the business fails it could wipe out your savings. You have to be prepared for that. If a whole family is involved, everyone in the family must be prepared to take that risk and have enough self-esteem to live through failure as well as accept success.

Is your family prepared to take risks? Some families would choose security and a steady job rather than take a risk—even though the risk might pay off better than a job working for someone else. Would you be prepared to help your parents start all over again if the home business didn't work out? Or are you more interested in making sure that you get some new clothes, some new records, and possibly a car when you're 16? It's important to know these things about yourself no matter what you plan to do.

Then you really have to know the market that you are going to get into. Who is your competition? What can you offer that will make people come to you? If you will need outside supplies, where can you get them and how much will they cost? Can they be delivered on time? How? Is the cost of doing your business likely to rise sharply? Can you raise prices enough to take care of new costs? If you have to borrow money to get started, will a failure mean that you'll lose your house and car? Is everyone prepared for that kind of starting-all-over-again loss?

Every step you take has to be taken on the basis of a clear understanding of why your product and service can attract people—and on a clear understanding of just who and where those customers are!

Also, there has to be a clear understanding of who in the family is going to take responsibility for which part of the enterprise. And you also have to decide how decisions are going to be made. Will one person be the boss? Will everyone be expected to discuss things? Does everyone get to vote? If one person is absolutely opposed to doing something, will that be enough to stop it? Things like that aren't bad things for a family to talk about even if they aren't going into business together. All of those things are important in the everyday life of any family.

The matter of money and how to share it if or when there is a profit is equally important. Does everyone get an equal share, no matter what they do? Is that okay because, after all, it's a family business? Is it important to distribute the money on the basis of how much people contribute to the enterprise? Will that mean that one member of the family might become jealous of another one?

That last question could be crucial not only to a family business but to the development of any kid's character. People who criticize other people because they make too much money—no matter what they do to make that money—often are people who think they deserve things for themselves regardless of what *they* do or how hard they work. When they see someone who is successful they may say that it's all a matter of luck. They just won't admit to themselves that someone else has more talent or works harder. That sort of negative characteristic gets in the way and is not likely to help anyone be part of a truly successful and creative life. Whether it's a family business or any other kind of enterprise, people who are jealous of other people's success are likely to be a drag to themselves and those around them. The best characteristic for a productive, creative life is to stop worrying so much about what other people are doing or not doing and to concentrate, instead, on what you can do and how you can do it better.

Again, thinking about these things is important for any family, whether they go into business together or not. Just being a family is an important sort of enterprise in itself. And the things that make a business successful are also likely to make a family successful as well.

In 1984 Phyllis Gillis, in her book *Entrepreneurial Mothers*, made some suggestions for simple steps that could be taken to see how children could be involved in a home business. If you ever discuss a home business, you might see these suggestions as being concrete things you could contribute.

"Get the children to do some of the following jobs for you:
— Answering the phone, taking orders.
— Preparing your product; if you bake apple pies, let the kid peel the apples.
— Helping with simple jobs, like stuffing enve-

lopes.
— Helping with deliveries, picking up supplies, counting the merchandise.
— Showing them how to do the bills.
— Making commercials, like on tape recorders.
— Designing your logo, brochure, or stationery.
— Cleaning up after you do other work.
— Talk out your problems with them; sometimes kids have an interesting perspective."

Here's another way you could figure out the possibility of your own family ever going into a family business.

Think of all the things that were mentioned about getting started in a home business. Would your family even want to discuss such things? Do you discuss doing things together anyway or do things just happen when a parent wants them to happen? Or do things happen when the kids become a big enough nuisance that they get their way just to keep them quiet? How do you feel about taking risks? Suppose the business failed and you had to move to some other neighborhood, changing schools, changing friends. Does that sort of change frighten you? Does it frighten your parents? If so, then together you need to decide whether the risk is really worth it to you. As a matter of fact, you need to discuss together the whole idea of change, whether you can handle it, what alternatives you have if things don't work out. Even the smallest successes don't come easy.

Actually, this matter of change is crucial in every aspect of life. The sort of change that a home business can make for a family is a sort of change that could be reflected throughout the entire society.

Alvin Toffler, a writer who has specialized in looking at the important factors that shape the future, made some very interesting observations on working at home in his 1983 book *Previews and Premises.*

Here are some of the things he had to say:

"People who will be or are working at home aren't illiterate workers just off some feudal manor. They are sophisticated workers, and they may, in fact, be able to use home computers, video and telecommunications links to organize new networks, 'electronic guilds,' new professional associations, and other forms of self-managed or self-protective groups...

"The electronic cottage, far from isolating people, may bring fresh life to these communities as home-workers fan out at night to participate in local groups. If home-workers had fewer social ties in the office or factory, they may have much closer ties with their families and communities...

"Without doubt, the single most anti-productive thing we do is to shift millions of people back and forth across the landscape every morning and night. A waste of time, of human creativity, of millions of barrels of non-renewable fuel, a cause of pollution, crowding, etc...

"The industrial revolution wrenched paid work out of the home and put it into factories and offices. That transformed society. It altered family life. It led to the transfer of education out of the home. It created the whole ridiculous pattern of mass commuting. It shaped our cities and our lives. This suggests that any transfer of work back into the home will carry significant changes as well."

Here's an example of a family business that certainly does look like a glimpse of the future.

Robert Dunlap and daughter Rachel, now 13, started R.E.D. Productions with $25,000 and their garage as an office. They make short, general-audience animation films to show on foreign networks in place of commercials. Rachel showed herself to be a talented writer at eight-years-old, so her father lets her concentrate on the artistic side of the operation, while he handles the financial end.

They couldn't find anyone who was willing to back an operation which allowed a kid to do the writing, so they used money her father had made from some acting jobs. They set up the shop so that most of the work — drawing, music, processing, camera work — is handled by the two of them with six part-time nonunion assistants. The films are being used in 78 countries, and also as short cartoons in American kids' programs. Each film costs about $2,000 to $3,000 per minute, not including labor and publicity. "The quickest return we have had on a film is six months, but the longest took about three years before we broke even," according to Rachel. They recently completed an hour-long show for PBS, entitled "Impact Earth." They said producing films for children ensures a continuous market for their work. They are reluctant to talk about their income, but according to an article in *Nation's Business* magazine "they are well on their way to at least $3 million by 1989."

Gary Patterson, who is in the oil exploration business in Wichita, Kansas, has a variation on a family business that might be of interest to any young person whose parents already have a business of their own. Some parents just don't want to let their children know anything about their business. Some children don't want to know anything about it. Families like this are divided up into compartments. The parents do one thing. The children do something else. They may not do much together.

But listen to what Gary Patterson has to say about an entirely different way of parents and children sharing things:

"With regard to my family and business situation, my goal is to establish a work ethic for my children. I want them to understand that the benefits of life and the ability to buy articles of need or desire are obtained through hard work and dedication. I'm attempting to accomplish this in two ways with my two children [Ryan, 12 years old, and Laura, nine years old]. I hire them on a part-time basis to do typing, expense keeping, data entering on the computer, copying, envelope addressing, bill paying and any type of job they are capable of learning. They have a time sheet that they fill out whenever they start working. They get paid by the hour and the same wage we would have to pay any other person to do the same work.

"My wife and I have also just formed a new business in which the children will be officers. In order to share in the profits of this company everyone must do their part. I think that the children are excited about this.

"This not only meets the goals that I have set for the children, but it builds self-confidence in them and gives them a strong sense of self-worth. They like, as we all do, being able to enjoy the fruits of their labor."

Some parents might not think that their children would want to do such a thing. But if you happen to like the idea, you might use Gary Patterson's idea to help talk to your own parents about letting you work with them. Or if you have another relative or a close friend with a business of their own, you might want to suggest some work that you could do.

All of this could be a stepping stone to a business of your own.

But think also of the other important things that can happen when kids and parents work together. Every member of the family has a chance to learn to respect the other members of the family because of what they can do and not just because they are younger or older. And, best of all, the children and the parents talk together more, share more experiences, become closer as a family. What a bonus!

Even talking about the possibility of a family business can bring a family closer together and let each member learn more about the hopes and character of every other member. There was a time when it might have seemed strange to talk like that, but we all know that today, in all too many cases, the members of a family can be almost like strangers to one another.

But suppose that a family decides that a business involving every member of the family *is* the way to go. Exactly which way should you go? The answer will be different for each family.

The first question to answer might be "Is there anything that every member of the family is interested in?" Suppose that every member of the family has been interested in sports. Maybe a sporting goods store would be an ideal family business.

Any sort of retail business could offer a chance for the entire family to work together. There are always chores to be done around a store that even very young children could help with—stocking shelves, keeping things clean and tidy, delivering handbills to advertise things.

Suppose that every member of the family has been interested in working in the garden. Perhaps a landscaping business would be ideal. Or a greenhouse.

As with a regular retail business, a service business of just about any sort offers opportunities for every member of the family. A family, at home, is a service industry in a way. If things are going smoothly, each member of the family has chores to do, each member does things that help all the other people in the family. Working just as hard at a family business just adds another, but not a new, dimension to your life.

Suppose that pets have been of interest to the entire family. Perhaps a pet shop or a cleaning and grooming service or a kennel or raising show dogs or cats would be the right way to go.

Suppose that every member of the family likes camping. Perhaps running a guide service or planning tours or running a special travel service for campers would be a good way to go.

The point is that you could start to think about a family business on the basis of the *things that interest the family most.*

On the other hand, suppose that the purpose of starting a family business is just to have a way for the family to stay close together, to work together, to not have to dash off to outside jobs, and to provide a business that can take care of the children when they grow older and have children of their own.

Then, the first step might be to decide which things you absolutely *wouldn't* want to do, so that you don't waste time thinking about them. Then you probably would need to start a careful study of what you could *afford* to do, what goods or services are needed where you live, or what goods and services are needed somewhere else where you all might want to go.

You would need to do a very careful study of the

market. Actually, it would have to be a lot more careful than the study you might make of a business just for yourself. After all, if you start a business while you are still living at home, the possibility of failure is not as bad to think about as if the entire family was out on the limb and depending absolutely on a single business.

Not every family business would have to be full-time, either—just as your own business would be part-time while you are in school.

A family business could involve just working on weekends or in the evenings or just one evening a week or one day over a weekend. The possibilities here are endless.

Every one of the businesses mentioned earlier could be done on a reduced scale as a part-time family business. You could just agree to groom or clean a couple of pets a week. You could just raise enough plants to sell on a weekend. You could just arrange one or two special camping trips a year.

On a part-time basis, a family business might just be an expanded version of something that, otherwise, you would do all by yourself.

If you or any member of the family, for instance, is interested in woodworking, you might make fine wooden toys for sale at craft fairs or even by mail order. If they sold well, the entire family might have a chance to get involved as the demand grew.

Your whole family might agree to paint someone's house. You might decide to get started on such projects by actually painting, for free, the house of an elderly or handicapped person who couldn't afford to pay for the work. You would not only learn a lot about painting, but you would certainly let your neighbors know that your only interest in life isn't making money. The idea of doing some of your work as a charitable act for someone who needs it can be applied to anything that you tackle. Charity, for a believer in the free market and in free enterprise, is a better solution to the needs of the poor than a welfare program.

Sometimes a thing that is begun just as a charity can lead to a regular business. Many families contribute homemade candies or baked goods to the sales of churches and other organizations. If your family's candy or baked goods always seemed to be the most popular, you could consider a part-time and eventually a full-time baking business as a family project.

Upholstering furniture is something that every member of a family can learn, usually, at a nearby vocational school or through adult education classes at night. It's also something that is in steady demand and that can be done easily in your own home.

Garage sales are something that an entire family can work on as often or as seldom as they please. You could have a sale once a month, once a year, or whenever. You might take on the job of finding things for the sale. One way to find things would be to attend auctions and try to buy things for very little that you could sell for a little more. Or you might just be the one in the family that stays alert for things in the house that aren't being used and which could be sold at your garage sale.

It's easy to imagine that a few successful yard or garage sales could lead to trying your hand at buying, refinishing and repairing, and re-selling furniture.

The formula for finding the right thing to do always is the same, however. Is it something you can do? Is it something you want to do? Is there a demand for it? Can you do it in such a way that your costs will be less than your selling price—in short, can you make a profit?

Full-time or part-time, having the whole family involved is just another aspect of the basic idea of doing useful work.

But the main point is the same as when you think about a business for yourself. The main point is that if people are determined to do something, if they have strong reasons for doing it, and if there is an honest market available to support what they want to do—THEY CAN DO IT. You can do it. Your family can do it. This doesn't mean that every family would want to do it. It just means that the possibility is there. The rest is up to you.

7

INVESTING
TIME
AND DOLLARS

Money is a green tool. It is useful. And, like any tool, its usefulness in the long run depends on the skill of the user.

People who consider money as an end in itself, as something they just want to accumulate, aren't likely to use the green tool very well. They might not want to take risks with it. They might want to hang on to what they have rather than use it for what they could do.

You are certainly not too young to decide how you feel about money. The fact that you are interested in making money rather than just having your parents give it to you is a strong signal that you understand, already, that money also is a reflection of your own self-image and self-confidence. You think that you can do things that are worth something. That's about the same as saying that you think that you are worth something. And that's a good feeling.

But money is an amazing tool in that it can be used to make things, and it also can be used to make more money.

Let's suppose that you have decided on a way to make some money. You have covered your costs. You have sold goods or services. You have some money left over, some profit.

You'll probably want to use part of it to make your business bigger, stronger, and better. You'll probably want to use part of it to buy something that you want, personally, or to do something that means a great deal to you.

If you're really thinking ahead, however, you'll want to make sure that some of the money is put aside for emergencies and the future.

The money that you spend on your own business is an investment in your work. The money that you spend on yourself is an investment in pleasure. The money that you put aside is an investment in the future.

There are, basically, two ways to invest money. One way is just to save it. A savings account in a bank is an example of that. It means that the money will be there if you ever need it.

There is another way to invest it. You could risk it by investing in someone else's business. Many businesses, and almost all big businesses, sell shares of stock in their company. If you buy a share of stock in a company, you get a piece of paper. But what you are really buying is a part of that company. You have become a "part owner" of that business. That's how a lot of companies get started, by selling off interests in the company itself. As a shareholder in the company, you will make money if the company does, but you can also lose money if the company is not successful. It is a risk, just like starting your own business.

But even after the company has used all the money that it got from selling the original shares of stock, those shares of stock are still circulating in the economy. There

is a big business just in selling those shares of stock. If a lot of people want the stock of a certain company, the price goes up. If people start selling those shares and there aren't a lot of people interested in buying them, the price goes down.

Sometimes a stock that can be bought for very little will start to go up and up because of some development that means that the company is going to make a lot of money. If the company does make a lot of money, it usually shares some of it with people who own the stock of the company. That's called paying dividends.

Someone who had spent just a couple of hundred dollars buying stock in a company like the Ford Motor Car Company, when it started, could be a multi-millionaire today just from the increased value and the dividends of that stock.

On the other hand, you could have invested in some other automobile company that went broke right away, and you would have lost all your money.

Kids with some extra money might want to start to learn about the stock market and how to risk money in it in hope of making more. There are books aplenty on the subject in your public library. There are stories about it every day in the business section of the newspaper.

But, unless you have decided to make the buying and selling of stock your entire life's work, you should think about a real danger in getting too involved with the stock market while you are so young. If there is other work you want to do, you should be concentrating most of your energy on that—and not on the market. To really know what you are doing in the buying and selling of stocks, you have to spend a lot of time working at it. But it probably would be a very good idea to spend *some* time investing in or at least trying to understand the stock market.

For one thing, if you learn about the ups and downs of big companies, you may get some valuable insights that can be applied to your own smaller company or work.

But you should remember all along that buying and selling stocks is a form of gambling, unless you have all of the sorts of inside information on a company that would make buying its stock a sure thing.

This isn't to discourage gambling—after all, in a way, you are gambling or betting on yourself whenever you try to do anything. It is to remind you that, particularly when you're young, investments in yourself and what you want to do are the best investments of all and will continue to pay steady dividends throughout your life.

A good mixture for your personal investing might begin with, first of all, a savings account. And don't forget to shop around at all of your local banks to find the one that pays the best interest on savings. There are so many different savings plans these days—and they keep changing—that just comparing them will be an education for you in economics, in doing research, and in taking personal responsibility for getting the information on which to make an important decision.

The second step might be to buy a share or several shares of stock. Buy one share of stock in a dependable, steady company. You may not make much money off that share of stock, but you will get the company's annual report, and you'll have incentive to learn how they do business. Then buy a share in a new company that might be a lot riskier but can give you insight into some new field and into how a company either succeeds or fails.

Someone might get the idea that it would be just as smart to buy a lottery ticket as to buy stock in a company about which you know very little. Both would be a gamble wouldn't they? Yes, there would be a gamble but there is a great deal of difference between taking the trouble to at least find out something about a company on the stock exchange and just trusting to *blind* luck in a lottery. People who get into the habit of lottery-type gambling (horse racing and so forth) often are people who seem to believe in magic. If only luck would come their way, all their problems would be solved.

When you buy stock you at least are believing in something more solid than that sort of magic. You are showing belief in the worth of people who try to produce things successfully. Win or lose, you're better off developing habits and interests like that.

There is an old saying that time is money. It means that a certain value can be attached to all of your time. It doesn't mean that every second of your day has to be spent making money. It means that you make choices about how to spend your time. If you choose to make money, then that part of your time certainly is money. It is time spent making money. But the time that you don't spend making money has real value, too. You could say it is spent in a different sort of "money"; in the value of learning things, in the value of having time to think about things, in the value of doing pleasurable things that make you feel better, in the value of helping others. In the value of being with people you like or love.

Perhaps you could think of the 24 hours of every day as the most valuable "currency" that you have. You can't have more than 24 hours in any day. You are on the most strict budget when it comes to that time. Your decisions on how to spend that time are the most important decisions you make every day.

The investment of your time is the most important investment of all.

Every hour spent doing one thing is taken away from an hour that could be spent doing something else. Your time budget is hard and fast. You can't stretch it out. You can't borrow to make more hours in any day. You just have the time at hand.

Many kids love to watch TV. Maybe they don't think of that as an investment. They probably just think it's fun. But don't ever get the idea that watching the TV is free! You pay for every second of it with a second of time that could have been used doing something else.

This doesn't mean that you should never watch TV, but it does mean that you should think about the real "cost" of sitting there and watching the screen. Sometimes you may learn something from watching TV—but how often? So, this is time that you could have been reading a book or a magazine or the newspaper. You could be talking to your friends, making plans, perhaps talking about projects that you could undertake. You could spend time with your family, talking about what you've done during the day, what you hope to do tomorrow, and what the whole family wants to do in the future.

Or you traded off the time that you could be spending taking a long walk or playing sports that you enjoy and that make you feel stronger and healthier.

The point is to be aware that some people watch TV to relax, so they don't have to think, or even move. It can become a costly habit because it uses up much more time than some people realize.

Going to a movie isn't quite the same. It takes some planning. You may go with friends and have a good time eating a pizza afterward and talking about what you've seen. It usually seems like something special—and you don't do it every day.

There are people who may tell you that you shouldn't take life so seriously as to think of TV watching as "costing" you time from other things. Because you are young, they may think you should play and have a good time. They sometimes say that life is so serious when you grow up that you would be wise to avoid it as long as possible.

But, actually, the sooner you think about taking control of your own life, of being responsible for your own decisions—of budgeting your time so that you spend it the way that you find most rewarding—the better. The sooner you challenge yourself to think and to act like a responsible *individual*, the sooner you will start making sure that your life never gets so dull or so serious that you end up watching TV, because there isn't anything else to do, because you're bored or just sick and tired of what you do all day.

What does it mean when someone tells you to act your age? Maybe it just means that they want you to act the way they did when they were your age. Maybe it means that they want you to act the way they think you should. What about your feelings in the matter? The way you decide to act—whether it is foolish and wasteful, or whether it is practical and productive, whether it is dull or whether it is idealistic—the way you decide to act is exactly "acting your age." You are a separate and special individual. You are not your age. There is no law of man or nature that says people have to act a certain way at a certain age. The choice of ways to act, of how to act, is absolutely up to you.

If you want to act like someone else's idea of the way

a kid should act then you are more like a puppet, with someone else pulling the strings, than like a true individual.

One of the most important reasons for thinking as early as you can about the important matter of work and productivity and creativity is so that you can remain an individual all of your life and not dangle from someone else's strings.

That gets us right back to the matter of the most important budget of all—your time.

Try keeping track of how you spend your time over a couple of weeks. Write it down, like a money budget. See what part of your time-capital you spend on school, on going back and forth, on doing things that have to be done in the house, on taking care of yourself and your clothes and other things, on just hanging out, on playing games or sports, on reading or watching TV, and so forth.

Take a look at your budget when you get it all together. Was each thing you spent your time on really worth it? And how will you set a value to judge that worth? This should bring you face-to-face with exactly how it is that you want to live your life and what you consider to be important.

The fact is that one of these days you will have to start thinking like that—or risk never having your life under control. So why not now? It's not painful. It doesn't mean you have to stop having fun. It just means that you have to start being very aware of the most important budget you can ever make — the budget of your time. Try to remember, no matter how poor or rich you ever are, time is something that you can only spend 24 hours of in every day. Those hours are your life-time.

Maybe we should reverse that old saying about time

is money. Actually, money is time. Every dollar is earned by spending some of your time doing it. Make sure that the expenditure is everything you want it to be. All the money in the world won't do you any good when, finally, you run out of time.

If you never learn to manage your time, you'll probably never learn to manage or even make money. If you don't learn to manage your time, someone else will surely try to do it for you.

A major problem for many young entrepreneurs, young people in business—anyone in business, as a matter of fact—is the management of time. Learning how to budget your time is crucial in getting things accomplished. Unless you are prepared to spend the time needed to get an enterprise started and then to make it succeed, you might as well not even try. And unless you learn to budget your time, it will be just like throwing away resources or money. Wasting time can mean worrying about something you don't know when you could just as easily go somewhere and get the answer. Just worrying won't solve many problems. Getting answers, thinking about answers, will.

Wasting time can mean not taking advantage of the experience of other people. If you want to know something and you know someone who has had the experience to know the answer, you are just wasting time if you don't go right up to them and ask. The worst waste of time of all is just thinking that you can't do things like that. Don't think you can't do anything. Just go ahead and try it. The worst that can happen is that you'll get turned down or have to go somewhere else or to someone else for the advice you need. But it is a terrible waste of time just to sit and fret and never try.

Wasting time can mean not thinking about things in advance. The more you think about your work, about what can go wrong, about what you might need, about where you'll get supplies, about where you'll get help if you need it, the more of those things you think about in the beginning, the less time you'll have to waste doing it later. Don't forget, when emergencies arise you are at a serious disadvantage when it comes to time—you simply don't have much. So the more you can prepare for in advance, the better.

If you take your time seriously, if you understand that time cannot be replaced, you will have taken one of the most important steps of all toward a successful life both in business and in the development of your own character.

There's something to watch out for, however. If you become obsessed with not wasting your time, if you try to run your entire life by a stopwatch, you might end up being as wasteful of time as if you were lazy and didn't care at all. Don't waste time worrying about wasting time. Try to make the budgeting of your time an easy and normal part of your life. Just be aware of the fact that time is precious.

Be aware that every hour spent one way means an hour that you can't spend some other way. Just as you shouldn't spend time counting your money over and over, you shouldn't spend time counting your hours over and over. You want to develop a healthy habit of budgeting both time and money. Watch out for it if the budgeting ever gets to be a pain in the neck. That probably means you've gone too far and need to back off a bit.

Time and money are both tools. Precious tools. But you have to be the boss. These are tools that should make your life happier, not miserable. Don't let any "things" become so important in your life that you have a feeling of being out of control or being forced to do things that make you nervous and even sick. Millions of people have struck a happy medium when it comes to time and money. You should be able to also. The idea of being independent and self-reliant is to make that more possible.

Even when you start making money, you should keep in mind that the value of what you do cannot be measured just in dollars and cents. It still has to be measured in terms of your time—of your life-time. Sometimes you may decide that a profit in extra time is as good as a profit in money. At least you should always be aware of keeping your budget nicely balanced between the money you need and the time you want to spend in the ways you decide to spend it.

Long before you have the problem of deciding what to do with your extra money (or time) you are going to have the problem of deciding how to get enough money to get yourself into business in the first place.

Perhaps the simplest way would be to ask your parents for the money. But that might not be the best way. It wouldn't teach you much about the way you might have to raise money later on to start another business. You'd come closer, if you did decide to borrow from your parents, by making sure that you offer to pay them a fair rate of interest on the money that they loan you—at least the same amount that they would get if they had left the money in the bank.

That's important for two reasons. First, it will show your parents that you are serious about your idea of earning money and that you understand the value of money. Second, it will force you to figure the costs of your enterprise the way any other businessman would have to figure it. The cost of capital to get started is a very real cost and one that you cannot ignore.

There is another way to borrow from your parents or even from friends and other relatives. You could offer to sell them shares in your business. For every dollar they lend you now, you might say, you will let them have a share of your profits after the first year. Each dollar, for instance, might entitle them to 10 or 20 cents of your profit. That would be like 10 or 20 percent annual interest. If they wanted to, they could hang on to their shares and keep getting that return as long as you made a profit. Or you could buy the shares back from them and not have to pay the dividend next year. Of course, if your business looked like it was going to be good over a long period of time, they probably would want to keep their shares and get the dividends.

What would happen if your business went broke? In regular stock purchases, when a company goes broke, the people holding the stock just lose their money. Sometimes they might get a little bit back, depending on the arrangements made as the company goes broke. You could do the same thing by letting your "stockholders" know that if you went broke you'd try to pay them back some part of their investment, or you could all agree to take a risk so that if you went broke that would be the end of it. Even there it all depends on the sort of deal you make. And it depends upon agreement between the individuals involved.

If you want to learn more about regular bank loans, even though you are too young to take one out yourself, you might talk to your parents about going to the bank with you and taking responsibility for your loan. It could be interesting to talk over your business plan with a banker.

There's another way to get the money you need that doesn't depend on anyone else but yourself. That way is to work at something until you can save enough to go into business for yourself.

But, besides earning money to get started on your own, a job of any sort—no matter how dead-end it might seem—will teach you some important things as well as provide money. You'll learn the importance of being on time, for instance. One of the toughest things that kids face when starting out in any business is convincing people that they can live up to their promises and that when they say they'll do something or be somewhere that that is exactly what will happen. Dependability is a crucial part of any business. Learning to be on time, every working day, even when you don't feel like it or when there's something you'd rather do, is one of the most important parts in building your own individual character.

The sooner you act so that people understand that your promise is "as good as gold," the sooner you'll develop the strength of character that will itself be as good as gold for your entire life.

A job that you take to save the money you need will also give you a close-up look at how other people do business. You'll be able to see customers and to understand how they act and what they want. You'll even be able to see whether the business you're working for manages its resources well or whether it wastes some of them. You'll begin to get an idea of what it means to have employees. In short you can learn a lot while you earn what you need.

You'll learn a lot about the differences in people too. Many young people are working to earn enough money to buy fancy clothes or have a good time on weekends. Some are working because they have to help their parents pay the rent and buy food. Some, because they feel that their entire life is going to be spent just going from one such job to another. The people who are there to help their families should have your respect.

Working hard just to buy something can trap you in a short-range way of looking at life. It means trading your life-time (remember our time budget?) just to have a few "things."

Remember, your goal in working there is to save enough money so that you can do something that you enjoy, something that will make enough money eventually to let you chart your own course in life just as you want it. Part of that course may mean a new car and nice clothes, a house, or whatever else you want. But the most important part of the course is that you will be steering it consciously and that the purpose will be the fulfillment of however you see yourself as an individual and not just as a shopper.

Remember, also, that you are working there so that you will never have to face an entire future of trying to get any job you can just to stay alive. You are working to save for the investment that will be the start of your life as a creative, self-reliant individual.

Keeping that in mind, the days on even the dullest job should go a little faster as you save up enough to get started on an enterprise of your own.

8

ARE
YOU A
VOLUNTEER?

There has been so much in this book about working to make money that you might think that capitalism and the free market is about nothing else. You might think that in a capitalist or free market society everything that you do has to be done to make money.

Nothing could be farther from the truth. Capitalism and the free market are mainly about choices—the freedom to make choices. There is the choice to buy something or not buy it. There is the choice to make something or not to make it. There is the choice to charge a lot for it or a little. There is the choice to work hard or to be lazy. There is the choice to try to make a lot of money or to be satisfied with just a little. And there is even the choice to do nothing at all if you can find someone else to take care of you.

But choice is the main thing.

And one of the most important choices in a capitalist or free market society is the choice to do some things without making a penny for doing them. You always have the choice to be a volunteer. You always have the choice to do something because you want to do it and not because somebody is paying you to do it.

This is such an important point that we are going to discuss it a lot in this chapter. It's a discussion about some of the most important points of all when it comes to the way you live and the world you want to live in.

It's very important to understand that capitalism and the free market are about a lot more than just money. They are about the way that you see yourself, the way you think about freedom, the way you think about good ways to live with your neighbors, and ways that you think would make the world a better place for everyone.

Let's consider one very special part of all that. Do you think that people should be left alone to make up their own minds about what they'll do or do you think that someone has to tell them what to do?

This doesn't mean asking if you think that people should be free to make up their minds to go out and kill and steal. Killing and stealing are things that one person cannot do without involving others. Killing and stealing must have victims. The only kind of killing that people could do all by themselves would be suicide. And there isn't any kind of stealing that people can do all alone. They have to steal from somebody else.

What we want to discuss here is whether people, in things that they can do all by themselves, or with other people who agree with them, should be free to do things or whether they should be told what to do. This is a discussion of things that are voluntary and of people who volunteer to do things. It is a discussion of the difference between being a volunteer and being someone who has to be told what to do.

A good deal of your outlook on life will be based on this question of volunteering to do things or being told to do things.

Did you volunteer to go to school? You may have wanted to go to school and you may still want to go to school. That's a different question. The question here is did you volunteer to go to school? The answer is that you did not volunteer to go to school. Whether you wanted to go or not you had to go because there is a law that says all young Americans must go to some sort of school, even if the school is operated in your home by your own parents.

Here's another question about being a volunteer or being forced to do something. Suppose that when you were very little, you had 10 toys. Suppose you knew some other child who didn't have any toys at all. Would you have volunteered to give that other child one of your toys? Or do you think that someone should have come along and taken a couple of your toys to give to someone who didn't have any? What about things that you have today? Do you think that it should be up to you whether or not you share them? Or do you think that someone should just take some of your things and give them to people who want them?

Let's think about different answers to those questions.

If you think that even going to school should be a voluntary action, you are at the far end of a spectrum of liberty. You probably believe that people should be free to do anything they want as long as doing it doesn't take away someone else's right to do what they want. You would believe in volunteerism. You would believe in a totally voluntary society.

If you think that, since school is good for you, everybody should be forced to go whether they want to or not, you believe in a society in which freedom has to take second place to things that the majority of people, or the political leaders, think is good. You wouldn't believe that people should be responsible for their own actions. You would believe that when it comes to important things like going to school, people need to be told what to do. You would not believe in a voluntary society.

What would happen in a voluntary society if someone decided never to go to school? They might never know how to do anything. They might never even know how to read and write. They might never be able to do any work.

Now, suppose you said that since it's their own fault, they should suffer for it. You would be saying that people make their own decisions in life and should be responsible for them.

But, still, we have someone who can't do anything. What are we going to do about that person? If you believe in a voluntary society, you might say that someone could, and probably would, make the voluntary choice to help that person. That's called charity. People throughout history have voluntarily been charitable to people who need help. On the other hand, if the person refused your help and just went off somewhere, you would have to say that they are free to do it and that you have no right to stop them as long as they aren't hurting you.

People who do not believe in a voluntary society would have another answer. They would say that the person was not responsible for his own actions. They would say that society is responsible. They would have a law that would take some of your money or your property and give it to that person. They would also have to have a law that would say that person would have to take the help whether they wanted to or not. That's called a welfare program.

Capitalism and the free market would count on

voluntary actions to take care of people who need help. In their absolutely pure form, capitalism and the free market would rely only on voluntary actions. Such a society would not have laws to make people do anything. There would only be laws to prevent people from stealing or physically hurting or killing other people.

But, as said earlier, there is no such society today. America comes closer than most but, still, America is a mixed society—with laws to control things people do and with welfare programs that substitute for charity.

As said earlier, also, your whole life is going to face you with decisions about whether you want your country to move more toward capitalism and the free market or move more toward socialism.

One way you can help move your country toward the free market is to be active in it yourself, to get into business, to take risks, to be responsible for your decisions, to not expect "society" to make up for your failures or to take away the fruits of your success.

Another important way to help is to do volunteer work that will show that people do not have to be forced to help other people and that good things can be done in your neighborhood and the world by people who are free and who volunteer and who do not have to be forced.

No matter where you live, you can find opportunities to do volunteer work.

And no matter what you want to do as an entrepreneur or as a scientist or as a poet—or whatever you want to be—you may find that volunteer work will help you.

For one thing you will make a lot of important contacts where you live. You will meet other people who believe in volunteering. Many of them will be people who have been successful in other work and now want to help those who really need help.

When you do volunteer work, as a young person, you take an important step toward convincing people that you are serious and dependable even though you may be very young. People who know that you are serious and dependable about your volunteer work are most likely to think the same thing about you when you undertake a business enterprise or anything else.

Suppose you are interested in making movies. You might volunteer to help your local little theater. They don't make movies, but they do create stage plays and what you learn there will help you later in your career.

Suppose you want to develop more self-confidence in dealing with people face-to-face. You could volunteer for fundraising drives in any of your local charities. The things you learn could help you later in dealing with people as customers.

Suppose you are interested in scientific things. There are many volunteer groups that are involved with monitoring pollution. Hospitals often have need for young volunteers.

There are volunteer groups in almost every neighborhood that help the elderly, teach people to read and write, care for the disabled, feed the hungry, and clothe the needy. No matter how young you are, you can learn important things about other people and about yourself by volunteering.

Best of all, you might find some need in your community that nobody seems to be taking care of. You might organize your friends, or your schoolmates, to tackle the problem. If you do it well, people will come to recognize you as someone who not only cares but who is capable of getting things done. That sort of reputation is exactly what you will need when you start seeking customers or support for your own enterprise. Or even if your plan calls for something altogether different, like being an engineer or a doctor or a minister, the work you have done as a volunteer will be of great interest to any college where you apply.

Here are some examples of volunteer activities by kids around the country. They may give you some ideas to use in your own hometown.

One of the largest and oldest volunteer programs involving teens is the Teens in Public Service (TIPS) program in El Paso, Texas. About 1,000 students from all over the city take part in the 10-year-old program. The teens volunteer in nursing homes, hospitals, churches, school playgrounds, and tutoring programs.

The project is a joint effort of the local newspaper publisher and the United Way.

VOLUNTEENS is a program started in Tallahassee, Florida. Sponsored by the local Volunteer Center, the program uses school service clubs to recruit teens for volunteer action.

Teens volunteered to decorate Christmas trees for senior citizens who still live at home but are unable to physically put up trees. The teens went back after Christmas and helped take down the trees, also.

The program recruits teens by contacting members of school service clubs and by placing ads in school newspapers.

A new program was started at Public School 36 in New York City. Called "Integrating the Concepts of Volunteering into the Elementary School Curriculum," the project was designed to help kids aged six to nine understand who were volunteers in their lives and why the kids themselves might want to become volunteers. The project began with the school's 2nd graders.

The class showed kids how they could become volunteers through existing programs and ways they could be volunteers on their own.

Volunteer groups (Guardian Angels, Jewish Guild for the Blind, Big Brothers, etc.) came to the school and spoke to the kids, and the kids also went to places where the volunteers worked. Later in the program the kids themselves volunteered at school and at nursing facilities. They also discovered ways to volunteer at home, such as cleaning, babysitting, and other small chores.

According to the class teacher, Elizabeth Capifali, "Children in the early elementary grades are at a stage in their development when they are seeking praise and acceptance outside the family unit. This stage of development offers an excellent opportunity to instill good positive esteem through community pride and involvement."

April Waters, 12, of Ruxton, Maryland, loves to read. When she found out that kids at the nearby St. Vincent's Center for Child and Family Care, an orphanage, didn't have many books, she decided to do something about it.

She began a campaign to get book donations from companies, libraries, friends, and neighbors. Books came pouring in. For her efforts, April won a $5,000 Care Bears Care-a-Lot Award. She plans to put some of the money aside for college and spend part of it to buy shelves to hold the books at St. Vincent's.

An essay contest on volunteerism was held at Jefferson Davis High School in Houston, Texas. The following are excerpts from the winning essays:

By Sandra Flowers, age 18:

"Volunteerism is loving to lend a helping hand to others when they are in need. It is also sharing your support and not accepting a reward...

"Volunteerism in all aspects is wanting to help aid and support others who are in need of someone's assistance, but not doing it for profits. When you volunteer your services, you do it because of a strong desire from the heart and soul to help others, and then you receive your reward from within your heart."

By Ricardo Ayala, age 15:

"People who volunteer don't get paid, but they get the experience and the emotion of helping people. The benefit is for everybody.

"The volunteer learns how to do things, and the other person gets the aid. Volunteers feel they are doing something for the community, for the people, for the country and for the world. Another benefit is that they make a lot of friends of different kinds."

By Tracy Burries, age 18:

"I know there are millions of teenagers today with nothing to do—wasting time in the streets. They can really learn a lot from being a volunteer.

"Volunteering doesn't ask for your money, only your time."

By William Richardson, age 16:

"Volunteering makes me feel good about myself— by being helpful, contributing to someone's happiness, exercising my talents. It makes me feel needed, wanted and independent."

9

EDUCATION, EXPERIENCE, AND ENTERPRISE

Some people think that education is what happens inside of schools. An entrepreneur, an "adventure capitalist," shouldn't think that way. An entrepreneur knows that if you are alert you can learn something wherever you are, whatever you are doing, and whenever you are doing it.

Thinking that education just takes place in schools would be like thinking that business only takes place in offices. Business takes place everywhere. It is in the mind of the person who plans or invents something. It is in the pictures and persuasions of advertising. It is in store windows. It's everywhere there's something to sell and someone to buy.

It's the same with education. The most important part of education is your own mind:

- If you are curious.
- If you always ask questions.
- If you always want to find answers.
- If you think a lot about better ways to do things.

If you are that kind of person, then your education goes on every minute of your life wherever you are.

But part of the time, unless your parents teach you at home, you are going to be in a school.

The most important skill that you can learn in the usual sort of public or private school is the skill of reading. By now you should be good at it. The fact that you're reading this book certainly suggests that you not only can read but that you are interested in reading.

It is just as important that you be able to write clearly. If you actually understand things, then you should be able to describe them by either talking about them or writing about them. The importance of writing is that it usually is more exact than speaking about things. It also means that what you have to say can be shown to many people and that you have a record of it.

What's this got to do with starting an enterprise? A lot. If you have a plan for a business venture, you should be able to describe it exactly. Writing about it helps remind you of things you may have left out. It encourages you to be complete in your plans. And if you want to get anyone else interested in what you plan to do, it is essential that you have it all written down. If you want to work with other kids, it is also essential that you and they are very clear about who is going to do what and when and why. Writing it all down is a way to make sure.

If you want to advertise your goods or services, you should be able to write down clearly why people should buy from you.

If you haven't had the opportunity to write much during your time in school so far, you should start right now to make up for lost time.

Start writing about what you'd like to do. Write about the way you feel about what's going on in the world. Write about the way you feel about what's going on in your family. Let other people see what you write. Make sure that what they understand is what you meant. The

more clearly you write, the more clearly they'll understand.

Read a lot, too. Read about people who have done the things you want to do. Read about everything that interests you. You'll learn a lot about clear writing when you find that some things you read are easy to understand while others are hard and may not make any sense. Don't blame yourself if they don't seem to make sense. Maybe they aren't written well. Try to see the difference between the kind of writing that keeps your interest and lets you understand and the kind of writing that puts you to sleep.

And don't ever get fooled into thinking that just because something is hard to understand that it automatically is very important. It may be. But it also may be just poorly written. Or worse—it may be that the author is trying to cover up some sloppy thinking with a lot of scholarly language.

At any rate, being able to write clearly is very important.

The Committee for Economic Development, a private business and education organization, recently surveyed 438 big businesses and 6,000 small businesses to find out what sort of mental capabilities were considered the most important in business.

The most important thing was a "high level of literacy." That means being able to read, and to understand what is read, and being able to express thoughts clearly by the spoken word and in writing.

All along the line, in this important survey, communications skills were at the top of the list, ranking above specific vocational skills. That just means that knowing how to think clearly, read well, and express yourself is more important than knowing how to do some particular job well.

The fact is that if you think clearly, read well, and can ask sensible questions, there isn't any particular kind of work that you couldn't learn to do!

For those who plan to be in business for themselves, this is even more crucial than working for some business where you might get by with knowing just one particular job very well. Being in business for yourself means understanding anything that comes along, being able to take advantage of every sort of information, being able to think of new and original solutions to problems, of being able to create goods and services that nobody else has thought of.

You have a basic responsibility for your own education. No matter what the schools teach you, you have the responsibility to make sure that you develop your mind as fully as possible. Often this means going beyond what the school has to offer.

Learning to program a computer will help you develop the habits of careful, logical thinking. Reading about successful businesses, about scientists, about inventors, about artists will help you understand those kinds of human activity.

Some schools, for instance, teach a lot about politicians but not much about merchants and scientists. Yet, you may discover if you study independently that scientists and merchants have done more good for the world than politicians.

Learning to apply mathematics to your own everyday life and to your own plans for doing things is an important way to broaden your education.

Learning another language, particularly if you ever plan to do business in the international markets, can be very important.

Art is important, among other things, because it tells you a lot about changing cultures and tastes—and an entrepreneur has to take such things very seriously.

You probably listen to a lot of music already—but maybe just to Top 40 tunes or to some particular kind of rock. That's very important for what it tells you about other people like yourself. But always remember that other people listen to other kinds of music. Knowing about their music should be important also. Most important of all would be trying to understand how music, like almost everything in our public lives, is part of business and merchandising, of finding audiences, of designing products for that audience.

You'll hear a lot of political talk also. Try to remember that you have a personal responsibility to think about what is being said rather than just taking it at face value. Just as you should be careful to avoid contradictions and saying things that don't really make sense in your own life, you should be careful to spot them in political statements. And you should be able to see that politics, like music, has become very much a part of the entertainment industry.

Text books often treat politics as something special and apart from ordinary life or business or entertainment.

There are some terribly serious things that you have to think about when it comes to schools.

One is whether going to college or getting practical experience would provide you with a better education for what you want to do.

If what you want to do is connected to some particular skill such as engineering or any of the sciences, or with some particular form of art, you might want to go to college and even graduate school, learning all of the techniques that possibly could be learned. If you plan to work for other people and not just for yourself, or if you think that you'll have to have a regular job to accumulate the funds for going into business for yourself, you may feel that having the proper credentials from a college is essential.

If you don't have a clear idea of what you want to do, there is a particular form of college education that should interest you. That's a liberal arts education. It means an education in which you study the arts and literature and philosophy, but also study the major scientific disciplines such as mathematics, physics, biology.

For either a career working for other people or a career as an independent entrepreneur, a liberal arts education has definite advantages.

First of all, it is suited to the fact that very few people stay in one job all their lives these days, the way their parents or grandparents may have. This means the possibility of constant change in which having a special skill may not be as important as having the mental attitude and ability to learn new things quickly and effectively.

A report in *Fortune* magazine has shown that 38 percent of corporate heads in the 1980's were liberal arts majors. At the same time, the *New York Times* reported that nine of the top 13 executives at International Business Machines (IBM) were liberal arts majors.

The Columbia Broadcasting System has funded an organization to investigate why liberal arts training is valuable to the American corporation. The proposition on which the group will work is that "in an increasingly competitive, internationally oriented and technologically innovative society, successful executives will be those

who can understand—and interpret—complex relation-
ships and who are capable of continually reconsidering
assumptions underlying old operating practices."

A study at Northwestern University has shown that
major companies plan to increase hiring of liberal arts
grads by some 20 percent in the late 1980's.

Lynne V. Cheney, chairman of the National Endow-
ment for the Humanities, has expressed public concern
about a study conducted by the Carnegie Foundation
which shows that many young people are choosing college majors, and careers, not according to their interests,
but instead choosing fields that promise to be profitable.

Cheney suggests looking at the future in ways other
than in terms of figuring starting salaries. First, because
few people today stay in the same job for an entire lifetime.
Also, it is hard to determine what skills will be in demand
five years from now.

Therefore, Cheney suggests that the best career
preparation is one that emphasizes general understanding
and intellectual curiosity: "a knowledge of how to learn
and the desire to do it." Literature, history, philosophy,
and the social sciences are the traditional majors believed
"to develop such habits of mind."

And the same flexibility of thinking, the same sort of
curious, risk-taking, change-taking mind is also the kind
that is well suited to being in business for yourself.

None of this is to say that if you are very interested
in a special subject such as engineering, an art, a science,
or anything else, that you shouldn't try to specialize in it.
The point really is that you should shape your education
around what you really enjoy doing and not around some
idea that this or that sort of course of study may lead you
to a job with a good starting salary.

A starting salary isn't where you'll spend the rest of your life. You have to think about the possibility of many changes in your life and not put yourself in the very dangerous position of getting stuck with only one thing that you know how to do.

Also, in the spirit of this book, you should always think long and hard about the possibility of working for yourself rather than for a salary.

It used to be that a salary meant security. That's not true anymore. Jobs come and go very quickly these days. Somewhere along the line you are likely to have to be responsible for your own future. In a way, you're always "in business for yourself" whether you work for someone else or not.

But what about the question of getting out of school altogether and just starting to do whatever it is that you want to do?

For some kids this is the very best course to follow. They've figured out a business. They're willing to take a risk. If they succeed, they can afford to go to college later on—to study exactly what they want without any pressure of studying things that they think might lead to a job. If they fail, they can always start over again and decide, then, whether to go to college or not, or to just try another business.

It's up to you. It's up to the exact definition—by you—of what you want to do; and it's up to you to make the sort of careful pro-and-con balance sheet about this that you would make about a business.

Actual experience in the commercial world is as likely to be impressive to other people in that world as a college degree, anyway.

And the earlier you can get that experience, the

better. Among other things it will better equip you to analyze whether you should go for an entrepreneurial life or go for college, whether you want to take risks on your own or whether you want to work for someone else.

You need to keep one other thing in mind when it comes to your education. There is a good deal of education, particularly for managerial, administrative jobs as well as for production-line jobs, that actually is teaching people to do things that machines can and will do better.

If there is any job, from bookkeeping to supervision, or from maintaining inventories to working a machine tool, that a machine can do better, you can safely predict that, in fact, a machine is going to do or already is doing it.

Be very careful that any educational decision you make does not mean you will be learning something that a machine can do better. The fact is that one of the great growth areas for any entrepreneur in today's world is to figure out ways for machines to replace human labor.

What does this leave for humans to do? It leaves the most exciting work of all—the work of being creative, of being able to solve problems that machines can't even understand. It means having those wonderful flashes of intuition that lead some people to design things for futures that no one else has predicted. It means painting pictures, inventing things, relating to people on a personal level, making music, exploring, discovering—doing all of the things that people *can* do that machines can't do at all or can't do nearly as well.

There is one form of education that a lot of people overlook: apprenticeships.

In the past, apprenticeships have usually meant learning some craft skill by working with a master craftsman. And for anyone who wants to do such things, it is still a superb way to learn. Let's talk about that first and then discuss a way you might turn an apprenticeship into something brand new, something good for a young entrepreneur.

There are programs that offer apprenticeships in over 425 occupations. Most are sponsored jointly by employers and labor unions.

Apprenticeship teaches all aspects of a trade. It helps the apprentice learn to work with different kinds of people in an actual shop. It familiarizes them with the overall picture of a company's operation and organization.

The competition to get in an apprenticeship is high. The work can be technically hard and physically demanding. Apprentices must show they are learning the task or may be dropped from a program during the probationary period at the beginning of the apprenticeship. Also, beginning apprentices may feel their work is menial or boring, and more advanced apprentices may feel that their pay is less than what they could earn elsewhere with their skills.

The minimum allowable age for an apprentice is 16 years, but most programs set the minimum age for entry at 18 because of company insurance policies. The maximum age varies among programs but, as an example one program set 27 as the maximum age for a carpenter.

Although about 60,000 openings occur for apprentices each year, over 200,000 people want to get in them. In the construction trades alone, an estimated eight applicants are qualified for every opening.

The availability of apprenticeships in an area depends on four major elements: economic conditions, labor union activities, the willingness of employers to train skilled craftworkers, and new technology.

Unions strongly support the apprenticeship system. By limiting the number of apprentices, unions can limit their members' competition for future jobs.

Some technological advances displace skilled workers and, therefore, greatly reduce the need for apprentices in those trades. However, new types of apprenticed trades are emerging that may fill the demand of interested applicants. As an arm of the U.S. Employment Service, Apprenticeship Information Centers (known as AIC's) serve as clearing houses for information about apprenticeships.

But what does all that mean for a young entrepreneur? It means thinking about a version of the apprentice system that might help you. It means looking around for someone who is busy starting new businesses and asking if you could apprentice with them for a while to learn how an entrepreneur operates. You might have to do the dirty work around the office, but you could still have an opportunity to keep your eyes and ears open and to learn what's going on. It also means that you might think of any job in terms of whether you could learn something from it to help you become an independent free enterpriser later on. Instead of thinking of it as just a job, you could then think of it as an apprenticeship—an on-the-job way to learn a certain skill or way of doing business.

There's even a way for a young entrepreneur to look at the traditional apprenticeship system and find a way to use it as a step toward going into business yourself.

Here, for instance, are some of the skills listed in the state of Virginia as being available for apprenticeship training: floral designer, greenskeeper, sailmaker, commercial photographer, optician, tool designer, topographical drafter, and many, many more including those you might ordinarily think of, such as electrician, mechanic, carpenter, baker, etc. Here's a list, in order, of how those routine apprenticeship skills could be turned to entrepreneurial advantage:

The youngster who has an idea for a novel chain of flower shops, the kid with an idea of a new kind of country club, the person who sees an entrepreneurial opening in catering to yachtsmen, the kid with something new to offer in the way of family or business photographs, someone who might be working on a mobile frame and glasses service, an inventor, someone with an idea of how to turn special maps of people's property into a business, a kid with a yen to do custom lighting and wiring for estates and mansions, a youngster who sees some service missing for local car owners, a kid who wants to buy and redecorate old houses, and someone with an idea of how to make a mint with specialty cookies or cakes.

Remember, an entrepreneur, no matter how old or young, is someone who can look at the world and everything in it with a completely fresh point of view.

If you're in high school you might find a teacher who is sympathetic with your hope to be an independent and creative producer in the marketplace. Perhaps you could work toward establishing an actual course of study in the school for others who may have the same ambition. In the directory section of this book there are many places where you can go for help in working out such a program either as a formal school activity or as an after-school activity.

The possibility of using your time in high school to your own entrepreneurial advantage can best be imagined by looking at an actual and successful high school program that already exists.

Several North Dakota high schools have formed a High School Entrepreneurs Club. Through it they establish what they call School-Based Development Corporations. And what an education they provide!

Their objectives and goals are to:

1. Provide new educational opportunities and dimensions by exploring self-employment as an option and being involved in the entrepreneurial process.
2. Create opportunities for students to pursue entrepreneurial activity.
3. Create jobs in the local community by utilizing resources of the school.
4. Establish a network between students, community businessmen and leaders, and high school faculty to maximize opportunities to start new businesses.

The outline of the program lists these points:

1. Create public awareness of the School-Based Development concept.
2. Form a School-Based Development Corporation, a local steering committee of community citizens to work for the betterment of the program, be a resource, and give guidance to the program.
3. Form a High School Entrepreneurs Club, recruit interested students, elect officers, appoint committee chairmen as needed, etc.
4. Involve entrepreneurial activities in school programs and issues of concern in the school.
5. Explore products or services that might have a market in the community or region.

6. Conduct market feasibility studies on these options to determine the most profitable one with the largest market.

7. Develop a market-oriented business plan that describes the business and includes detailed information on the product or service, the market, the people required, supplies and suppliers needed, costs, space requirements, and the financing needs.

8. Develop with the appropriate public agency dealing with small business, or with the appropriate private small business organization, an organizational structure for carrying out the business plan and resolve any legal or liability problems that could arise from operating the business.

9. Secure the financial resources for the start-up of the business.

10. Begin start-up operations, including establishing business control procedures and hiring students.

11. Operate the business and resolve operational problems, being patient since new enterprises need time to prove themselves.

12. When it's successful, sell the business and prepare to repeat the entire process with a new plan and new participants.

13. Use profits, if any, from the sale to benefit the school and to start the next business.

Here's how the Associated Press reported on the North Dakota plan and some other similar ones:

"Teen-agers in several rural North Dakota communities will be starting their own businesses through a project designed to save small, economically depressed school districts and towns from extinction....

"Under similar programs, students in three Arkansas school districts opened community newspapers and rural Georgia students started running a feeder pig operation.

"The projects stimulate development in dying rural communities and give students job experiences they otherwise could not get, officials say...

"[*One of the school districts*] which has 185 students is considering using its kitchen to make frozen pizzas for wholesale...

"[*Another district*] plans to start a business raising bedding plants, providing a market study shows it would have a local market...

"School districts cannot start a business that would compete with one existing in their communities, and the businesses are supposed to be self-supporting..."

Even earlier than high school there are countless opportunities for even very young kids to work out a school-based entrepreneurial education venture. At the Hunt School, in Hunt, Texas, the fifth and sixth grade classes formed a corporation that has tried such one-shot businesses as bake sales and barbecues as well as manufacturing actual products. They've been taking in between $15,000 and $25,000 a year in the process. After paying all their expenses, they've used their profits to buy such things as band instruments and sound systems for their school. After students have participated in the program for a full year, they share in an annual out-of-town trip financed out of the company's profits—and completely organized by students. As one teacher put it, "These kids know more bankers by their first names than

I ever did. They'll look anyone in the face and shake his hand." And, commenting on the annual trip, he said, "They've found that hard work and being polite and dependable can take them to [*a resort hotel*] where they can eat steaks for a week."

Whether or not you can use your time in school to start such a program or be part of one already existing, there still are all of the "educational" opportunities of part-time work, of independent study, of weekend businesses, and so forth.

But even beyond that, the responsibility will be yours for discovering and studying those things which will make you a thoughtful person, able to analyze things, able to make decisions and evaluate consequences. In the last part of this book there is a long section written especially for parents that talks a lot about education and about the development of a self-reliant personality. If you take the trouble to read it, as well as suggest that your parents do, you may find a lot to talk about in your home and with your family about exactly the kind of education for exactly the kind of life you want to lead.

Finally, there is the question of home schooling, of not going to a school at all, but learning with your parents. About a million kids were doing it in the mid-1980's. Many of them were the children of deeply religious people who didn't trust regular schools to teach the spiritual values that are important to them. But there were others whose parents were determined that their children become self-reliant and self-determining, learning to think for themselves. Home schooling is a complicated and very demanding decision for any family to make. If you want to think about it, you need to start some strenuous research work at your local library to discover the laws about it, to find people who have done it, to understand its advantages and its problems. Two of the best one-stop sources of information on home schooling are a newsletter called *Growing Without Schooling*, 729 Boylston St., Boston, MA 02116, and the Hewitt Research Foundation, Box 9, Washougal, WA 98671.

Whatever sort of schooling you are involved in, here is a checklist of things that you could insist on for yourself, no matter what the particular school emphasizes. It's a checklist that you can apply to any sort of schooling.

If the schooling actually helps you achieve these things, fine. If not, you have to strike out on your own, or with your friends and family, to make sure that you develop these traits.

You want to develop a sense of your own individuality. You want to be able to evaluate yourself. That self-evaluation is as important as any report card you'll ever get.

You want to learn to think for yourself, to be critical without being rude or a show-off or a pest. You want to understand things and not just take an adult's word for everything. Unless you actually understand something and unless it really makes sense to you, you should hold off on believing it. You should be prepared to draw your own conclusions even if you draw one that isn't popular or approved.

You want to be able to say what you think, clearly and without embarrassment. You don't want to go along with the crowd just because that's the easy way.

You want to learn to say no when your friends press you to do something that you really don't want to do. No matter how much they might kid you for sticking to your guns, you can take comfort in knowing that real strength is doing what you think is right and real weakness is going along with the gang. Wimps go along. Strong young men and women chart their own courses.

You want to understand that your behavior is yours to control, not society's, not some textbook's rules. You make the decisions about yourself.

If you are doing things that aren't working out—you can change. Reject any ideas you may hear that you are a victim of society or that people just have to do certain things whether they want to or not.

You want to know deep in your heart that you are responsible for your own decisions in life. You have to think them through. You have to be responsible for getting the information that will help you make the decisions. Don't let anyone, or any book, including this one, "educate" you away from being responsible for your own life. Listen to all the advice you want, learn everything you can. But remember that in the long run, you are responsible—for you.

10

LAWS, LIABILITY, AND LICENSES

Like anyone else who is trying to do something productive, young people trying to run a business have to learn about laws that make doing business difficult. They have to learn about liability (which just means the danger of being sued for doing something if someone thinks it hurt them). They have to learn about licenses, which are ways that various levels of government try to regulate business or collect money from them without calling it a tax. They have to learn about taxes in general. They have to learn about zoning laws and a lot of other red tape.

Just as you are never too young to be productive, you are never too young to start thinking about the many ways that non-productive people try to tie down people who are productive.

Throughout your life, your attitude toward these things will have a lot to do with whether these things get better or get worse.

Many laws, which slow down business or try to make businesses behave the way politicians think they should, were passed because one or two businesses got into trouble. Politicians, who are always on the lookout for something to do that will make them seem to be protecting the public, jump on any case of a bad business and pass laws that treat all business as bad or, at least, as possibly bad. The fact that a business which wants to be successful over the long run has to behave itself or lose its customers isn't enough for the people who like to pass laws. Passing laws, you might say, IS their business. Since politicians don't produce any material things, they try to get votes by passing laws that help some people, even if they hurt others.

Very often, when a law gives something to one bunch of people, it has to take it away from some other bunch.

Suppose that some people want to spend Sunday without having to see any stores that are open. For them to have that "freedom," they have to take away the freedom of businesses who want to stay open on Sunday and the freedom of people who want to shop on Sunday. There are laws exactly like that.

Suppose that some people who have businesses don't want other businesses to charge less for their goods or services. They get politicians to pass something called a "fair trade law" which means that you can't sell your stuff for less than someone else. This provides "freedom" from competition for the stores who want laws like that and it takes away the freedom of people who want to give bargains to their customers.

There are so many laws that try to say what businesses can and cannot do that only the most skilled lawyer can even keep up with them.

If you are a young person just getting started in a business, the best thing to do might be to just ask other businesspeople in the town, or your parents, or friends of theirs, if they know of any law against what you want to do or how you want to do it. Even if they say there is, you might want to talk to a lawyer just to make sure. There might be a lawyer who would be willing to offer help to a young person voluntarily.

One good thing you have going for you as a kid trying to get into the free market is that a lot of older people are going to admire your spirit and want to help. They see so many kids who have no get-up-and-go at all. They may really be excited by one who has a lot of it!

On the other hand, there a lot more people who don't want kids to do much of anything. Young people have a tough time trying to get anything done. There always seems to be someone who is trying to stop them. Some people try to stop them by saying that kids should act like kids and just play and go to school. Some people say that kids are too young to be trusted. Some people just say that kids shouldn't work.

There are several reasons why people say that kids shouldn't work. We've mentioned some of them earlier in this book, but there's one we haven't mentioned that is very important. Some older people figure that young people might be willing to work for less money or work harder than the older people. To protect their jobs these older people support laws that keep kids from working.

Just to give you an example of the sort of thinking that you may be up against, the country's largest association of labor unions, the AFL-CIO, made a big issue out of opposing a proposal to hire 15-year-olds to work for private businesses operating in national parks. They said that "at the age of 14 to 16, youngsters are not merely smaller workers, they are still maturing physically and mentally...40 hours a week cleaning motel rooms, mowing lawns in the sun, or even doing dishes...is a bit much."

But a union official also said that it "would take jobs away from older workers and expose youngsters to exploitation." That last part means that the union official doesn't think that kids are smart enough to make up their own minds about whether they are getting a fair deal or not. What do you think?

Fortunately for kids, most of the laws against kids doing any work are written to prevent people from *hiring* them to do work. Those laws don't apply to a kid who wants to go into business for himself.

But that doesn't mean that there aren't a lot of other laws that a kid has to watch out for.

For instance, kids do not have an absolute right to keep their own earnings. Because kids have the legal right to be supported by their parents or guardians — including food, shelter, clothing, medical care, and education — the reverse also is true. That means that parents have the right to the services and income of the kids.

Kids, however, can make sure their income is their own by getting a written agreement with their parents that the income will stay the property of the kid, or if the kid works for some time and the parents do not take any of the money, they cannot suddenly start taking the child's wages. This should very seldom be a problem, but it is a law.

Kids do have to pay income taxes. But just like anyone else, they have the right to keep those payments to an absolute minimum. And if they earn less than a certain amount they don't even have to file a tax return. In 1986, you could earn up to $3,500 and not have to file, but the figure keeps changing, so you'll have to check. The tax information that your parents get each year will tell you all about it.

Kids have the right to open a bank account in their own name. Kids may deposit and withdraw money from an account without the consent of the parent.

Generally, kids do not have the right to make contracts. Contracts do not have to be written to be legal. They can also be oral, or spoken, and still be valid. In most states contracts are not binding if one of the parties is a minor. The fact that it is not binding does not mean the contract cannot be performed by both parties, but it does mean that kids can "disaffirm" or back out of the contract. But minors *can* enforce contracts against an adult, and therefore many people are hesitant to sign a contract with a minor without the parent's or guardian's signature. If a child does "disaffirm" a contract, he or she is not allowed to enjoy the benefits of that contract at the same time. For example, if a kid contracts to buy a bicycle, then disaffirms the contract, the bike must be returned, and the kid must pay for whatever use he or she has gotten from the bike.

Some contracts kids make are void from the time they sign the contract. Leases are void contracts when signed by a kid, and in some states marriage contracts are void if either of the signers is a minor.

Some contracts are binding and *not* subject to a minor's disaffirmation. Examples of these include:

1. Contracts made by minors in the course of their own business, provided the contracts are fair and reasonable.
2. Contracts made when entering the military.
3. The contract made when a minor signs a driver's license.
4. Contracts entered into by a minor for loans or insurance.

Also, if the kid must contract with someone for

"necessaries" such as food, shelter, medical care—because the parent is not providing these to the kid—then the contract is binding.

Kids do have the right to own real estate, but they do not have the right to manage or control the property. The kid cannot rent, sell, or manage the property—that control is in the hands of the kid's parent or guardian.

The age of majority is the age when a kid is viewed as an adult in the eyes of the law. Each state determines its own age of majority, but in most states that age is 18. At the age of majority, however, kids are not given all of the rights of an adult. For example, the drinking age may be higher than 18 for kids. States have the right to set the age qualification for numerous activities, and kids should check the laws in their state to determine what those qualifications are.

Insurance is another thing to think about because there are so many liability laws these days which encourage people to sue other people at the drop of a hat. Many people think that these laws are really out of hand and that there are many of them that go far beyond just protecting people from harm.

According to Jerry B. Partlow, agent for J.V. Arthur, Inc. Insurance of Winchester, Virginia, in most cases liability will fall back on the legal parent or guardian for kids under the age of 16. Homeowners' policies will usually cover the liability for a kid's business, but there is such a diversity of possible jobs for kids that each case must be considered separately.

Two considerations for kids starting their own business are the labor laws involved in kids hiring other kids to work for them and the worker's compensation laws which are different in nearly every state.

When a kid starts a business, there are three different liability problems the kid should be concerned with:

1. *Premises and Operations*—if someone is physically injured on premises or as a result of the operation.
2. *Products and Completed Operations*—if the kid sells lemonade and someone later becomes ill from drinking it, for instance.
3. *Personal Injury*—for example libel, slander, or false arrest, but not physical harm or damage.

For a kid with a business in some states, all of these areas would be covered by the parent's or guardian's homeowner's policy. But it's different from state to state. Another problem is that not all parents have homeowner's insurance. Many people who live in apartments, for instance, do not have policies because they don't feel they need them.

Partlow suggests that if you are going to start a business, your parent should discuss the particulars with an insurance agent in your state and make sure about the liability laws.

Here's what this one insurance agent wrote, in detail, about the matter:

"It does seem that there would be a substantial amount of interpretation by various insurance carriers as to the potential responsiveness of the liability section of a Homeowner's Policy for a minor's 'business activity.' The definition of business activity is extremely vague, thus it would be extremely important that the parents obtain a written interpretation from their carrier prior to allowing the child to engage in a business activity.

"Another alternative is to have the Homeowner's Policy endorsed with a Business Pursuits Endorsement.

This would clearly define the business activity and acknowledge the assumption of risks by the insurance carrier.

"With the various liability and worker's compensation exposures faced, it would be very difficult to make a general statement about the insurance issue. A suggestion that the insurance issue be resolved by a professional insurance agent prior to engaging in the activity would certainly be advisable."

Maybe things like that simply won't be of concern to you, but keeping them in mind is always a good idea since it better equips you to deal with the world as you get older. Also, if you are looking for support from older people in getting your business started, they are likely to want to know if you have thought about all these things. Knowing that you have might make them more willing to help you.

You should also give some thought to whether you should form a legal corporation to carry on your business. At the start, most home businesses just operate as what is called a sole proprietorship. That means that just one person owns the business and is responsible for it all. When a corporation is formed, it means that the corporation is responsible and that its liability is limited to the amount of assets (money or things) that it owns. Talking to a friendly lawyer can help you decide what you should do here and, again, the fact that you look into it and know about such things is likely to make people to whom you might go for help or backing think more highly of you. Besides, the more you know about business and the red tape that business has to deal with, the better off you'll be no matter what kind of work you intend to do. Above all, it will get you used to the fact that productive people always have to be aware of, and protect themselves against, the many political barriers that are erected to protect some people or businesses against other people or businesses.

You will discover, for instance, that laws are generally stacked against people trying to get into business. Some people who already are in business actually use politics and the law to try to prevent competition. Entrepreneurs, who are individuals trying to do things for themselves, often have to fight against established businesses as hard as they have to fight against politicians. Thank goodness that they still think it's worth it! We are all better off because they do!

One of the biggest things that government can do to benefit one group of people while penalizing another group is to enact zoning laws. A zoning law just says that the local politicians in your town, city, or county can decide who can do what in any particular place. Suppose that the people in a particular neighborhood don't want anyone to have a business in that neighborhood.

In a really free society they would have to make sure that everyone who wanted to keep businesses out got together so that they owned all of the property in that neighborhood. Because they owned it, they could decide exactly what to do with it. But, of course, they would have to be responsible for spending the money to make sure that they owned all the property.

Instead of being responsible, like that, they could get together and beg the politicians to pass a law preventing anyone from having a business. If they could get the politicians to pass such a law, the people in the neighborhood wouldn't have to be responsible for what goes on—they could just call the police or the politicians if someone tried to have a business.

Zoning laws go way beyond that, however. In one of the richest suburbs of Washington, DC, the zoning laws even prevent people from having free-standing basketball nets on their own property. This means that people who don't want kids to have basketball nets can just call the police if some kid dares to have such a net. In a free society, people who hate basketball hoops, or kids, would have to be responsible for their prejudices and would have to buy all the property and then only let people who agreed to hate basketball hoops, or kids, into the neighborhood.

Just about anything that you want to do may run up against a zoning law. It really depends on your neighbors. If your neighborhood is zoned for residential use only and you started to make something in your basement, a snoopy neighbor who didn't like you could blow the whistle on you and ask the police to stop you from doing whatever you might be doing in your basement.

But actually, if you know your neighbors and if they like you, you are not likely to have any trouble with doing business in or from your own house.

You may not, however, be able to have a sign outside your house advertising your business. And you would have to be careful about noise and mess—but that's what a good neighbor would be careful about anyway, no matter what they were doing. And being a good entrepreneur is a lot easier if you are also a good neighbor.

Another thing to be careful about is having too many big trucks rolling up bringing you supplies. Once in a while wouldn't be bad, but all the time might really annoy any set of neighbors even if they are your friends.

Just be careful—and thoughtful—of your neighbors wherever you do business!

Business licenses are another way that politicians

make it difficult for people to do business. Actually, most licenses are just another excuse for getting money from productive people who work for themselves. Unfortunately, there just aren't many politicians who go very far out of their way to help business people. Most of them seem to feel that anyone in business, even a kid, is a fat target for new taxes, regulations, red tape, and money, money, money for the politicians.

Getting a license may never be needed for what you plan to do—but just as with zoning and insurance, you should know about it.

One thing to watch out for: if you apply for a license to do business in an area that is not zoned for business, you are likely to get the politicians down on you.

Perhaps the worst thing that politicians do to business people is make them collect sales taxes. Almost every state in the United States now does this.

Although there is a section of the Constitution that makes it illegal to force anyone into "involuntary servitude" or slavery, most businessmen in the entire country are forced, usually against their will and without any payment, to involuntarily serve the politicians by collecting sales taxes. It costs a lot of money to do this—with the cost being passed right along to the customers, of course. It takes a lot of time to do this. It's a pain in the neck, but you will have to check your local regulations about whether you have to collect sales taxes or not. Sometimes, if what you are doing as a business is just offering a service to people—like mowing lawns or babysitting—no sales tax is expected. But if you sell something directly to people, chances are you'll be expected to collect sales tax. Check into it, at least.

Does all of this sound as though it's just too much

trouble to go into business? Does it make you wonder why anyone would want to go into business when the politicians make it so hard for them to do anything? Well, no matter what the politicians do there are still millions of people who want to be in business for themselves and who will give it a try no matter what. And for those who do their work really well, and find a lot of customers, there's usually enough money to be made to keep a lot for yourself even after paying off the politicians with all their taxes and red tape.

Just keep remembering, it's productive people who make a country a good place to live. Thank goodness there are a lot of them—and let's hope that you'll be one of them yourself.

11

WORDS
OF
WISDOM

Thomas Edison, the inventor of the light bulb, the phonograph, and lots of other things that we use every day, was born in 1847 in Milan, Ohio. His father was a jack-of-all-trades, having worked as a tailor, well-digger, nurseryman, graindealer, lumber salesman, and lots of other occupations.

Tom had only two months of regular schooling, learning everything else from his mother. He loved to read everything he could get his hands on, having an intense curiosity about the world and its great men.

At age 12, he started working as a newsboy on the Grand Trunk Railroad of Canada and the Michigan Central Railroad, selling newspapers, books, candies, and other odds and ends. He started his own newspaper, the Grand Trunk Herald, and printed it himself on an old hand printing press right on the train. He was able to sell several hundred copies of his newspaper each week.

In 1905, for a book titled *Little Visits with Great Americans,* Edison was asked about what he was like, and what kinds of things interested him, as a child. Some of his answers might surprise you.

Question: Did you enjoy math as a boy?

Edison: "Not much. I tried to read Newton's 'Principia' at the age of 11. That disgusted me with pure mathematics."

Question: Were you anxious to learn?

Edison: "Yes, indeed. I attempted to read through the entire Free Library at Detroit, but other things interfered before I had done."

Question: Were you a book worm and dreamer?

Edison: "Not at all."

Question: What was your first work in a practical line?

Edison: "A telegraph line between my home and another boy's, I made with the help of an old river cable, some stove-pipe, and glass bottle insulators."

"I was never much for saving money, as money. I devoted every cent, regardless of future needs, to scientific books and materials for experiments. It helped me greatly to future success," Edison said.

"I never did anything worth doing by accident, nor did any of my inventions come indirectly through accident... I have always kept strictly within the lines of commercially useful inventions. I have never had any time to put on electrical wonders, valuable only as novelties to catch the popular fancy," Edison explained.

Another great inventor of the past was Eli Whitney, who was born in 1765. In 1793, when he was just 28 years old, Eli invented the cotton gin, a machine which revolutionized the agricultural industry.

In the 1894 book, *Men of Achievement, Inventors*, Eli's sister was quoted as relating the following account: "Our father had a workshop and sometimes made wheels of different kinds, and chairs. This gave my brother an opportunity of learning the use of tools when very young.

THOMAS
ALVA
EDISON

He lost no time, but as soon as he could handle tools he was always making something in the shop, and seemed to prefer that to work on the farm."

When he was 12 years old, Eli built a violin from scratch. Later when his violin was examined by experts, it was described as an excellent piece of work.

About the same time, Eli took his father's watch completely apart and then put it back together before his father could find out. The watch continued to operate perfectly.

At age 15 or 16, during the Revolutionary War, Eli went into business making nails, as well as doing repair work on machines. Eli worked alone at this job during the winter, and then worked for his father on the farm during the summer.

Eli came up with a plan for expanding his business, and he managed to obtain help from a fellow laborer whom he hired when he was on a short trip. During this trip Eli called at every workshop on the way and gleaned all the information as to tools and methods that he could.

In 1789, Eli started at Yale College as a freshman in order to get a "liberal" education.

Edison and Whitney are two examples of how successful businessmen and entrepreneurs started working and gaining valuable experience at an early age. Their stories are from a long time ago, though, and there are lots of successful businesspeople around today from whose stories we can learn lessons.

Most kids get advice from adults every day. It comes from parents, aunts, uncles, teachers, ministers, or just about any other adult you happen to meet.

Some of the advice is helpful, some of it isn't, and some you just don't understand.

We thought it might be a good idea to ask some adults, whom you might not get a chance to talk to yourself, what they were doing when they were your age.

The adults we asked are all successful business executives or entrepreneurs, and we specifically asked them to tell us how they first got involved in business when they were kids. Some of them told us what they did as kids that helped them later on in life, and some mentioned the mistakes they made as kids.

Many also agreed to offer you their advice on how you can prepare now for a successful business career. Some even have advice for your parents, which you might want to share with them.

We believe you'll find these comments useful and that they will make you think about how you can get involved in business and capitalism right now. But we also hope you won't forget that you have to live your own life.

You will eventually have to make your own decisions. But never turn down information and advice that can help you form your own opinions and that might help you make the right choice later on.

• • •

Malcolm Baldrige, the former United States Secretary of Commerce, was for many years chairman and chief executive officer of Scovill Manufacturing Co. Secretary Baldrige was also a member of the Rodeo Cowboys Association.

Secretary Baldrige said:

"As a youngster, I wanted very much to work on a ranch, and began when I was 14. By the time I reached college I had gained a good bit of self reliance. This proved useful when my parents reached the conclusion that they wouldn't be able to afford to pay for all three children to attend college. Since I was the oldest, I had to pay my own way—and I did this mostly by selling dry cleaning contracts.

"My experience as a ranchhand and as a salesman taught me that I needed to help myself before anyone else would help me. My work on the ranch especially taught me the value of perseverance, common sense, and hard work through long hours.

"Young people should not aim immediately for the ivory tower of the business world. Even if they are the boss's son or daughter and are destined to go far in the company, they need to understand a structure from the bottom up. As a foundation for future careers, they should study hard—not just computer science, but math, reading, English, communications skills, and so on."

Secretary Baldrige advises parents to "talk to your kids. Give them a chance to figure out their problem before you do it for them. This will instill self-confidence, which is the most important thing, and teach them problem-solving. They will soon learn that they have to come up with their own answers and not just look to mom or dad for a packaged solution."

• • •

Lillian Katz is the president and founder of the Lillian Vernon mail order business.

"I started working from the time I was 14 years old — my first job was at a movie theater where I worked as an usherette making 10 cents an hour. Then I went to work in Barton's Candy Shop as a salesgirl.

"Those jobs gave me an early appreciation of working. I realized then that work could and should be a pleasant and enjoyable experience.

"All my jobs involved working with the public, so I learned to deal with all kinds of people and to handle myself with all personality types. It also helped me overcome being shy—in my jobs I had to be outgoing."

Katz, whose corporation grossed over $100 million one year, advises young people "to give careful thought to what they like to do and what they do best. Since they are going to spend most of their adult life working, they might as well enjoy it—and be good at it. Everyone has different skills and abilities and you should choose a career that you can be good at.

"A career decision should not be taken lightly. Carefully think over your options and discuss them with your parents, friends, and your school guidance counselor. If you don't like what you are doing early enough in your career, make a change to something that better suits your needs and personality."

Katz offers the following suggestions to parents: "Give your children some responsibilities around the house to help take care of themselves, such as making their bed every morning. This will give them a sense of independence and a feeling of accomplishment. Teach your children the value of money. Give them a reasonable allowance—and encourage them always to save some money, to spend more responsibly yet also enjoy their money.

"Give your children a lot of positive feedback and re-enforcement when they do a chore well or bring home good grades. When they are good, tell them so—likewise if they are bad or let you down, they should know that too. Use guilt constructively, not destructively. Let them know you don't always expect perfection — but you do expect them to do the best they can. Be sure to point out their strengths and capabilities.

"Keep your fears to yourself — give your children confidence in life, people, society. Instill them with caution and prudence — but not fear! Most importantly, give your children lots of love! Tell them you love them as often as possible — and that you respect and admire them!"

• • •

Carl Helmers, of North American Technology, founder of the first mass circulation computer magazine, *Byte*, and a continuingly successful publisher of high technology journals, said:

"I was always a reader and forever inspired by books ranging from fourth grade level stories of Thomas Edison, P. T. Barnum, and the kid who discovered a volcano in his (Mexican) back yard, to later grade level readings of Tom Swift and his X, Robert Heinlein, and stories about mankind's quest for flight, for electricity, for understanding.

"Every kid should think about more than the spur of the moment. Dream about the future. The future could be next summer's vacation trip or getting a Nobel Prize or that first billion dollars. I was dreaming about space ships and satellites and going into orbit when I was five years old in the early 1950's. Of course I never did accomplish that—but then again I may yet do so.

"How many people actually do what they intended to do as teen-agers? Long range planning is important to the young at heart—of any age—but more for the activity of finding out about oneself. My plans have certainly

changed in the course of events. A rigid plan can hide
many an opportunity."

● ● ●

David Packard is the chairman of the board of the
Hewlett-Packard Company and one of the most successful, and richest, entrepreneurs in the world. Packard
reminded us that a great personal interest, and not the
desire for money, may be the most influential factor in
becoming a success. Packard wrote:

"I became interested in engineering at a very early
age, was intrigued by the existing developments in technology, and I started the company because I wanted to do
something in a technical field. I was not at all motivated
by wanting to be a capitalist, or even with the hope of
making a lot of money."

● ● ●

Richard M. DeVos is the president and co-founder of
the Amway Corporation, one of the most successful entrepreneurial enterprises in the world. DeVos is currently
listed on the Forbes 400 list of richest people in the United
States.

DeVos said:

"When I was young, I did many different odd jobs to
earn spending money: raking leaves, shoveling snow, and
anything else which I could find to do. However, my
grandfather was a 'huckster,' who delivered garden-fresh
vegetables and fruits to people in their homes. Oftentimes
he had left over items that I could sell and make a few
pennies. Later, I worked in a gasoline station while I was
in high school."

While he was growing up, DeVos listened to his

father. "Dad had two themes which he kept repeating over and over. The first was his insistence that I never use the word 'can't.' That negative word was a barrier to performance, and he showed me that there was usually a way to do something which I might have thought couldn't be done. The second was his advice to be in business for myself. Dad was in sales almost all of his life, and he lost his job through no fault of his own when I was a young man. He felt that owning one's own business (entrepreneurship) would put a person in control of his own destiny."

"The most important advice I can give young people today is to remember that you are a child of God, and have great self worth and potential. Building on that theme, it is important to set goals and work to achieve them. They can be relatively short term in the early years, but one must have a definite achievement in mind in order to perform to the best of one's ability. Whether it is higher grades, a place on an athletic team, or any other specific goal, plan to use your natural talents and time wisely in order to reach it. Then set another goal. Success in life is not one giant step. It is a succession of many steps, some successful and some not so successful. But each of the steps is a learning experience, enabling one to go on to the next step!"

• • •

Kemmons Wilson is the founder of the Holiday Inn motel chain and now president of the Kemmons Wilson Companies.

Wilson sent along his *Twenty Tips for Success*:

1. Work only a half a day; it makes no difference which half—it can be either the first 12 hours or the last 12 hours.
2. Work is the master key that opens the door to

all opportunities.

3. Mental attitude plays a far more important role in a person's success or failure than mental capacity.

4. Remember that we all climb the ladder of success one step at a time.

5. There are two ways to get to the top of an oak tree. One way is to sit on an acorn and wait; the other way is to climb it.

6. Do not be afraid of taking a chance. Remember that a broken watch is exactly right at least twice every 24 hours.

7. The secret of happiness is not in doing what one likes, but in liking what one does.

8. Eliminate from your vocabulary the words, "I don't think I can" and substitute, "I know I can."

9. In evaluating a career, put opportunity ahead of security.

10. Have confidence in yourself.

11. A person has to take risks to achieve.

12. People who take pains never to do more than they get paid for, never get paid for anything more than they do.

13. The more steam you put in your work, the louder you can whistle when your work is done.

14. Opportunity comes often. It knocks as often as you have an ear trained to hear it, an eye trained to see it, a hand trained to grasp it, and a head trained to use it.

15. You cannot procrastinate—in two days, tomorrow will be yesterday.

16. Sell your wristwatch and buy an alarm clock.
17. A successful person realizes his personal responsibility for self-motivation. He starts himself because he possesses the key to his own ignition switch.
18. Do not worry. You can't change the past, but you can sure ruin the present by worrying over the future. Remember that half the things we worry about never happen, and the other half are going to happen anyway. So, why worry?
19. It is not how much you have but how much you enjoy that makes happiness.
20. Believe in God and obey the Ten Commandments.

• • •

Dorothy E. Brunson is president of Brunson Communications, Inc., a corporation which owns a chain of radio stations including WEBB in Baltimore, Maryland. Brunson was one of the first members inducted into *Working Woman* magazine's Hall of Fame.

In *Working Woman* magazine in November 1986, Brunson explained that her family expected her to be a teacher or mother, but she wanted a different career: "I come from a black family, and it is hard for them to understand why my business success is important to me. They cannot understand a $10 million debt. You have to keep your distance from your family in that way because they may influence your business decisions out of the need to love and protect you from failure."

Brunson told us she "earned money as a child, primarily as a babysitter."

Brunson said she "read books, stayed in the library

and expanded my learning horizon." She said she became "A Jack of All Trades." Reading as a child helped her the most in her future work.

Her advice to young people is that "school is only the first level in learning. Nothing is unimportant; if you are going to do it, give it your best."

In *Working Woman* she expanded on that thought: "Structured education is not a means to an end. What I learned outside of school was just as important as what I learned in the classroom. I would emphasize to them [*children*] that knowledge comes from many places."

She advises parents to "teach your children ethics. Work and human ethics. People are the ultimate product that make you successful. Let them [*kids*] shovel snow on occasion."

One thing she regrets about her childhood is that she did "not gain confidence and self-assurance" until she was an adult.

• • •

Walter H. Annenberg is the chairman and chief executive officer of Triangle Publications, Inc., publishers of *Seventeen* magazine, *TV Guide*, and other publications. Annenberg is a former United States Ambassador to Great Britain and Northern Ireland.

Annenberg said:

"My advice to young people who are still in school would be that they not only concentrate on their work as students, but in addition to this, participate in school activities so as to strive for well rounded achievement. Frequently young people, unless they have urging and direction from parents, do not have the necessary experience to recognize the importance of participation.

"My advice to parents is that they have a continuing duty in policing their children in terms of education, decency and respect for the dignity of others."

• • •

Roland Halle is a film-maker and entrepreneur who won an Academy Award in 1980. As a young man, he set a goal for himself—to be a millionaire by age 40. He miscalculated a little, because at age 38 he was a multi-millionaire. He said:

"Financial success was important to me. It was a way to prove to myself that I could become somebody, that I could achieve my goals. I don't think I sought financial success for its own sake.

"I did not want to become a millionaire just so that I could live in luxury, not the extravagant kind of luxury, or so that I could have anything at all. But I did not want to worry about money and I didn't want my family to worry. My needs are few. I don't need a Cadillac or another big car, I have modest tastes. I don't think that will ever change because that's the way I was brought up.

"Money is not power. I think that the real power is the control over oneself. You can see people in power right now who have no control over themselves and that means they really have no power. I believe the only true power is that over one's life, control over one's life.

"I have always been very goal-oriented, which is to say that I would set objectives for myself, and on the whole I would always reach them, no matter how inaccessible they were to start with. I would succeed.

"When I dream of something that I want to achieve, the most important part is to think it through. I have to think about it very hard, I have to analyze exactly what it is I want. Only then I can chart the route that will take me there."

• • •

Tom H. Barrett is the president and chief operating officer of Goodyear Tire and Rubber Company. He has worked for Goodyear since 1953.

Barrett said:

"As I was growing up in Topeka, Kansas, I could hardly wait for my 12th birthday. I would be 12 and thus 'of age' to go to work in the family poultry processing business.

"It was not something that was planned. It just happened out of necessity. I joined my father and two older brothers at the plant and began learning the skills of the business...defeathering; cutting the wings, legs and breasts; packaging; preparing our product for the customers who would buy and consume it. You might say I was in manufacturing. So far as I was concerned, reaching 12 was reaching manhood. But it was not considered a big deal.

"There were 10 children in our family. All of the boys worked in the plant. The girls concentrated more on sharing the housework that goes with a large family.

"In the summer, the job was virtually full time. During the school year, I went to the plant after classes and put in a few hours after finishing my paper route. Most weekends and holidays were spent at the plant. These were the busy times. My father had a stroke at 50, and after that my mother and the boys really were running the business. I worked at the plant until I was through college and joined Goodyear.

"In those days, you didn't hear the term 'work ethic.'

At least I never did. Work was a way of life, a fact of life. I guess the closest I came to defining work ethic then was to think that people who didn't work much were lazy.

"Today, a strong work ethic, regardless of how it is achieved, is a strong leg up for an individual in any business, any occupation or profession. From what I've seen, people with a strong work ethic can pass 75 percent of the people in their field, even those who have an edge in background or education.

"Advancement does require some personal sacrifice. A strong work ethic accepts that. Desire to succeed just has to transcend some measure of comfort and convenience. A workaholic, of course, is an undesirable extreme. Somewhere between, there's the optimum balance that produces the competitive individual who finds satisfaction in work yet has time for the other things of life.

"When my wife and I were raising our own three children, all girls, we gave some thought to the early training and experience necessary to development of the work ethic. We didn't have a business to send them off to, but we did manage to expose them to the pleasure and rewards of productive endeavor.

"For example, all through their high school and college days, they were provided with such things as books, tuition, food and clothing, but earned their own spending money at tasks like waiting tables and working as a life guard. How much they earned determined how much they could spend for discretionary items like movies, records and makeup. Another factor is that the children were made a part of our work environment. They understood the sacrifices required for success.

"Looking back, I think my work load as a child and a youth was on the heavy side at the expense of things like social and sports activities. But if you met my wife, you would conclude my social life was very good.

"I think parents today are shortchanging their children if they fail to provide them with the means and incentive to gain early experience in what it takes to realize one's expectations. The baseball bat or doll earned today becomes the ability to earn a house or a car in later years. And the work ethic learned through early experience becomes a personal asset that lasts a lifetime."

• • •

William E. Dearden is the retired chairman of the board of Hershey Foods Corporation. He worked for the Hershey chocolate company from 1957 to 1985.

Dearden said:

"I had a 350 daily paper route from 10-12 years of age; then mother died and I was sent to an orphanage where I worked on a dairy farm until 18 years of age.

"I learned to depend on myself, and to work hard to achieve good marks in school in order to get a good job when I finished school."

Dearden said, "There were opportunities that I could have taken advantage of which I did not seize. One was learning to play the piano; another was learning a foreign language."

Dearden also had some advice for both kids and their parents.

For children he said: "Have a dream — work hard to achieve it. Nothing is impossible, but *you* have to decide what *you* want from life."

For parents Dearden advises: "Give your children an opportunity to think for themselves, but with good guidance on your part. Let them learn the value of hard

work outside the home early in their lives, thereby learning the value of money, self-reliance, and discipline."

• • •

Robert Anderson is chairman of the board and chief
executive officer of Rockwell International Corporation.
He also worked for the Chrysler Corporation from 1946 to
1968.

Anderson said:

"Success in business is rarely the product of good
fortune. It is sometimes the product of 'being in the right
place at the right time.' Usually, success in the free
enterprise system results from dedication, perseverance
and hard work—lots of hard work.

"Your ability to do well in business, however, also
depends on talents generated from within. In the fast-
paced excitement of the business environment, creativity,
risk-taking and independence of thought are all elements
of the entrepreneurial spirit which is the foundation of
American business.

"By combining all these elements with a sincere
desire to achieve excellence in every endeavor, you will be
assured of a place in the winner's circle.

"But it's important to start now. Work hard in
school, absorb as much as you can, participate in after
school clubs and activities, keep informed of current
events in the world, and pursue your special areas of
interest or hobbies. All of these activities are important in
the contributions they make toward our entrepreneurial
talent of tomorrow."

• • •

Z. E. Barnes is chairman and chief executive officer

of Southwestern Bell Corporation. He has worked in the telephone business since 1941.

Barnes earned money as a kid by doing lawn care work and having a newspaper route.

"I became competitive through athletics. I also went through the Depression and learned many lessons of hardship. I think this helped me develop a sense of relating positively to others," Barnes said.

But Barnes said he did make mistakes. "I did not work up to my potential as a student. I relied too heavily on the opinion of others."

Barnes advises young people to "Get involved! In school, in your community. Learn the true value of being of service to others."

Parents should help their children "with their education. Be patient *but* firm. Encourage them to think through their problems *before* acting. Stand aside and let them grow."

• • •

Howard S. Rich of Laissez Faire Books, the largest dealer in books about the free market, said:

"I knew I would be in business when I was five years old. I identified with my father who was in a small business.

"I sold comic books and on Halloween sold chalk to neighborhood kids. It was a different product from the kind available in local stores. On hot summer nights I carried used deposit bottles to stores for extra income.

"The chalk was an inventory problem. There was great demand for about two days and we had to walk two miles to get it restocked. On balance we underordered.

"My best advice for young people is to work in a

small business. The advantage is in being able to perform many different functions."

• • •

Pat Wagner of Pattern Research, Office for Open Network, a Colorado firm that specializes in putting people with ideas together with people who have resources to invest, said:

"I didn't earn money as a kid, but I was always doing projects of different kinds and I seemed to have a knack for talking other people into these projects. I liked to make something happen — like a play, where my best friend and I wrote the script, got the school to help us find actors, dancers, musicians, etc., and we did a nice show. About 100 folks were involved. And we sold out several performances.

"But business was evil. Everyone in my family who was in business was either a crook or a failure. However, my attraction to capitalism and business grew because I wanted control of my projects and I wanted to earn my own money to run them. I loved writing and wanted to publish books, so I learned how to be a printer. I wanted to find a way to help people communicate better in the village where I was living, so I started a newspaper.

"The desire for money was not foremost — anyone looking at our business books would have to agree. However, falling in love with the idea of freedom and the sacredness of the individual meant, for me, seeing business — the entrepreneur — as a way of putting wonderful things into the world. Poetry, theatre, music, dance, literature were put into the world not only because someone was creative, but because someone knew how to put these things into the marketplace.

"The best advice I have for parents is to let children fail. Teach them to see that — BAD NEWS IS GOOD INFORMATION!!! Mistakes are information, failure is information. Don't bail the kids out financially if they blow their money on something stupid, but do help them think through new ideas. If the kid chooses the wrong way and it is not illegal or physically dangerous, let them go ahead and try it."

• • •

Logan T. Robertson is a medical doctor in North Carolina. He said:

"As a teenager I was extremely fortunate to have a mentor who influenced both my personal development and, ultimately, my career. I was also fortunate to have parents who were willing for me to explore my interests and to take advantage of the special opportunity that was offered me.

"Dr. Charles Norburn, an exceptionally gifted surgeon practicing in Asheville, won my respect and we became close friends. When I was 16 he invited me to come during school vacations and share the bachelor's room he kept at the hospital, to work there as an orderly and to assist him as needed.

"He gave me every chance to learn about the practice of medicine and to actively participate in patient care. He included me on his numerous house calls as well as allowing me to observe surgery. He taught me the importance of listening to the patient and set a faultless example of honesty, integrity, kindness, fairness, and dignity.

"By his own attitude and behavior he inspired me to seek a high level of excellence in my own endeavors; he kindled a zest for life and a joy in accomplishment that was never verbalized, but which he emanated unflaggingly.

"Although I did not earn money, I did earn rewards of highest value. Those summers and holidays at the hospital propelled me happily through my teen years, on to Yale and Cincinnati School of Medicine and a life's vocation as a pioneer in industrial and preventive medicine that I am still enjoying at the age of 70. And 'Dr. Charlie' is still active and bright-eyed at 96...I visit him every week.

"I wonder if this 'non-preachy,' non-competitive kind of learning experience might not be a uniquely valuable way to teach youngsters not only practical skills, but also the self-confidence necessary to look at situations creatively, to develop new ideas and to act on them. The mentor-student relationship is certainly one which enriches both parties again and again.

"I believe there is more to capitalism than quicker and slicker ways to make a buck. The free market system, like any other system, is only as good as its components. Shoddy parts and dirty oil won't make an efficient machine."

• • •

Butler Shaffer is a California lawyer and a widely read writer on the philosophy of the free market. He offered the following advice for kids:

"I would say the same thing I would say to an adult: Do the kind of work in which you enjoy the work as an end in itself. In other words, to discover the kind of work you would perform even if you did not get paid for it, or, even where you had to pay to perform it. After many years in which I worked with management—as a labor lawyer—I have come to the conclusion that work that is performed primarily for the purpose of making money—or deriving any other side benefit (such as status, power, etc.)—will almost always drive the individual nuts (slowly or quickly).

"While 'money' is decidedly neutral, I strongly believe that the pursuit of anything—including money—is the root of most misery in our lives, because we end up doing things we really hate in order to get what we think we want, namely, money. The trick—and it is an easy one to perform—is to find the kind of work you truly enjoy as an end in itself, that is for its own sake, and then figure out how to best perform that work in order to make good money, obtain a good reputation, etc. Money, in other words, is a reward for doing things well — provided they are 'things' other people are willing to pay for—and you are more likely to do things 'well' — and enjoy life more —if you enjoy the work itself."

• • •

R. W. Bradford is a young, successful dealer in precious metals, in Washington state. He said:

"My first real income was at age 12, when I delivered advertising door-to-door, undercutting the post office rates. I would deliver a flyer about every six weeks, so the work was fairly steady.

"This easily eclipsed the money I made selling stuff door-to-door or delivering newspapers or shoveling snow.

"When I was 13, my brother and I convinced the local Coke bottler to lend us a large cooler and a local hardware store to let us use the sidewalk in front of their store during a local parade put on for tourists. We bought a few blocks of ice and cases of pop and were in business. We made $35 each in two days—very big money in 1961.

"The next year I was on my own and all sorts of kids were operating the same business on the same route, so I hired 'little kids,' meaning seven- to11-year olds, to load pop in their wagons and hawk it along the parade route. I made $75 in two days.

"The following year, I decided I needed a new product line: I expanded into popcorn and ice cream, but competition kept my profits down to about $75. The next year I operated my concession for the benefit of a volunteer group and used volunteer labor. We did pretty well.

"When I was 14, my parents decided it would be a good idea to operate an ice cream business so we kids could make money. My mother kept the books, my father negotiated the lease and the basic deal with the ice cream company. But the work was done by the kids.

"Before long it was evident that my brother and sisters saw the store only as a way to make a little cash when it was convenient. This enabled me to work very long hours (60-70 per week) and make even more money. I also quickly became the manager of the business, deciding such matters as changes in our product line and advertising.

"We did okay. When the books were settled, I made $1.15 per hour the first year and $1.40 per hour the second. I also learned a lot about the ice cream business both from practical experience and from reading books on ice cream manufacturing and marketing.

"I advise young people who want to be entrepreneurs to go out and have 'real world' experiences by going into business for themselves. There are plenty of opportunities for those who seek them. During my years in the coin business, I constantly did business with teenage (and younger) entrepreneurs who had become coin hustlers.

There are also opportunities in such divergent areas as sales and recycling. A kid has to use his eyes and his brain — the opportunities are always there.

"I think I wasted far too much time on formal education. After high school I spent four years at college. I was full of fire and lust for knowledge and spent a lot of time trying to convince other students and professors of some of my more peculiar beliefs. This was enjoyable, I suppose. But in the course of earning a degree, I wasted a lot of time.

"In retrospect, I think that I educated myself and that the college I attended did little more than provide me with a library, a few professors to argue with, and a means of avoiding conscription.

"I would have been far better off if I had taken responsibility for myself and gone to work or started a business much earlier.

"I think anyone, of any age, who wants to be an entrepreneur should have courage and try. In my own case, once I worked up my courage and decided to try running my own business on a serious full-time basis, I was immediately successful. The time I spent worrying about it, preparing for it, planning, etc., proved to be of no value. It was simply time wasted."

● ● ●

Michael E. North is a professional engineer. He said:

"Although I am not a Ross Perot type success, I am self-employed, with growing assets."

North offers the following advice: "Do projects for yourself, but learn to FINISH them, and as you get to 12 or so start searching out work opportunities. Many a self-employed or professional has a myriad of things they could use reliable help with, home maintenance, yard work, painting, snow shoveling, babysitting, etc. It doesn't have to be, in fact with government rules it probably won't be, a 'regular job.' Besides at a 'regular job' you must pay too many taxes."

• • •

Russell Kerkman is a successful electrical engineer in Milwaukee, Wisconsin. His early jobs were snow shoveling and lawn mowing, a paper route, and house painting during summer vacation. He has also been a janitor, a plumber's helper, and a carpenter.

"Besides the work experiences which provided that initial interaction with people other than my family, the fact that my parents encouraged my interest in mathematics and science was so important. My Dad sitting with me in my chemistry 'lab' in the evenings after a long day of work, but before he left for his second job, is vivid yet today.

"Although it may seem trite, the many sandlot baseball games I participated in taught me so much about people. There were those who had to win at any price, those who would belittle the less athletic, but also those who knew it was just a game. Funny thing is, those who saw the game for what it was turned out to be adults I am glad to know, while those who had to win seem to have faded in memory and importance.

"I think that young people, however, should spend less time in junior and senior high school participating in organized sports and, instead, spend more time on varied work experiences that expand one's understanding of people and the world.

"The best thing that parents can do for their children is to turn off the boob tube! Cast aside the idea of an allowance. Encourage children to work for what they get. Do not fall into the trap of many today who believe they are doing their kids well by simplifying their lives. The sooner they understand the real world the better.

"And, when youngsters get into secondary school, they should take advantage of the diversity of courses offered. If one is inclined to pursue one's education beyond high school don't forget to take shop. I didn't but, fortunately, my Dad provided opportunities for me to acquire some experience in the general trades. The contrary also exists. If college is not for you, don't hesitate to take a course or three in mathematics or the sciences."

• • •

Every one of those people is a different and distinct personality and even though their stories share many things such as a sense of self-worth and the willingness to take risks, the ways they went about their own activities in the free market were also different.

You are different from everyone else in the world also. We all share a lot of human traits but we all have our own mixture of them that is absolutely unique. There is only one you. No matter what lessons you may learn from the examples of others, you are still mainly responsible for what you do in and with your own life.

The best thing about a system in which people are free to trade openly and freely, and also free to own their homes, their tools, and their ideas and the product of their work and ideas—the best thing about such a system is that it is wide open to the infinite variety of human difference and human creativity. There is a place in such a system for you, a place that you can make for yourself. In some parts of the world you can find such a place only if you are born into the right sort of family. In other places you can only have a special role in life if you follow the right leader and recite the exact words of some political creed. But where people are free to trade, they also are free to find their own place in the world and to do the work they do best.

Not everyone does this, of course. Some people would rather never take a risk and they may feel a lot better always working for someone else. They want someone else to take the risks. Some people may not even want to think for themselves. They want someone to tell them what to do, when to do it, and even what to think. In a free society there is room for everyone. But the people who create, who have new and exciting ideas, who work hard, who work effectively, who do the things that need to be done and that people want done—these people are very special. They make the changes that affect our lives. Sure, there are people who don't like everything that is done. There are people who can give reasons for not liking some part of the free enterprise system, or even any part of it. They honestly think that if they could run things, they could do it better. They want the political power to do just that.

But somehow, over the years and across the world, the market system still seems to strike the best balance and produce the most good (and goods) for the most people.

You can be a part of that way of getting things done. You can be a part of it no matter how young you are. It's not a matter of age. It's a matter of spirit and of will. And it's a matter of your own very personal decision.

If you choose to work as an entrepreneur in our society, you will be involved with a lot more than just making money. You will be involved in making changes in the way people live. New inventions, new ways of working, new products, and new services always make changes in the way people live. When those changes are made in the marketplace, they at least can be made without violence, and if they hurt the environment or other people, they can be stopped by the customers themselves. People suing the makers of bad products or polluters have already done much to correct damages that can be done in a market economy. On the other hand, political changes often are accompanied by some sort of violence or at least involve the use of force against people to make them do what the politicians want.

In a truly entrepreneurial society change should be constant, just as in every part of the natural world. And, because the change is brought about by individual people, working at individual projects, the changes can be small and even experimental. The changes can be abandoned if they don't seem to work. They can be duplicated and improved if they do seem to work. A society that keeps moving on step-by-step on the basis of individual initiative doesn't have to worry about the huge shocks that can occur when, for instance, an entire government makes a big mistake.

There is a special advantage for your thinking about an entrepreneurial life at an early age. It will get you into the habit of understanding that life is constant and eternal change. You will not be afraid to change as the times change and as new information and new tools become available. You will never be caught in the terrible situation of people who think that they can just do one thing, perhaps for one company, all of their lives. When times change, when companies change, they often are left out.

They must rethink their entire lives and probably retrain themselves for work they never even imagined doing.

Entrepreneurs, even young entrepreneurs, know that every new day is a new challenge. They know that learning must go on throughout life. They know that learning is not just something you do in school. They know that you do it every day, with every experience, if you are alert and thoughtful. They know that the ability to think includes the ability to change, to adapt, to use new tools and information. Change, which may seem such a threat and a danger to some people, will just seem a challenge and an opportunity to the entrepreneur. Actually, this ability to see opportunity in change is such a human trait that it shouldn't be confined to any style of work or life, such as the entrepreneurial outlook. It is just that—a trait of human beings. It is natural. It is part of the natural world.

What need not ever change, however, is your own personal sense of self-worth and possibility. Skills probably become obsolete about every five to ten years in our fast changing world. But your personal principles and your own self-esteem, your own ability to think (rather than just absorb "facts")—these are things that are part of your inner life as long as you live.

Good luck! Or, better, Good work! Good thinking! Good life!

12

THIS PART
IS FOR
YOUR PARENTS

The proposition of this book has been, simply, to put in terms that young people can appreciate, the meaning of capitalism and the free market, to encourage them not only to understand it but to become part of it, to share its ethics of individual responsibility, and its rewards—and to do it while they are very young.

Your role, as an adult, can be crucial. You probably have it in your power to dampen some young person's creative and entrepreneurial spirit or encourage it. Either path is easy to take. Young people can be discouraged simply by lack of interest or a somber appeal to adult authority. Or they can be encouraged just with a warm and sincere "go ahead!"

There has never been a time in history or a place on the planet where there has been more wide-open opportunity for kids to shape their own future or for families to encourage the development of individual excellence of mind and character by their own lights and in their own ways.

The child without individual character or will, the drifting, thoughtless child is a child of choice—a child whose parents probably don't care or who feel that a child's character is best formed by outsiders, preferably professionals. The child with low self-esteem is another child of choice, forged from the abuse or coldness of parents. Such failed children may always constitute a sad majority, a potential underclass forever bowing to authority, scraping along, taking what they can, unable to make or create much on their own.

From one point of view, nothing seems to be going quite right for kids these days. Kids too often are given the idea that in school adults just want them to shut up, memorize some facts, and score well on tests.

Kids are often given strong indications that adults don't want them to work. Our laws, our labor organizations, and welfare groups contribute to this picture.

And what about trendy parents, who hook their kids up to earphones to learn French while they sleep? Or those who overwhelmingly seem to favor tennis lessons over having the kids do chores—much less actually make a buck on their own?

Television entices kids to become passive watchers instead of active doers—and many parents bless the tube for being the cheapest babysitter in town.

But there are many other sorts of children: bright, energetic, proud, and adventurous. They get out and hustle. They make stuff. They win the science fairs. They don't get bored; they get busy. They and their parents not only talk together but often work together.

As it has been throughout history, they will eventually make the discoveries, turn the dreams into material reality, sing the songs, write the glories, climb the mountains, create the wealth, and keep the planet a good place to live.

Even so, capitalism and the free market, the very

force that makes possible all the choices that parents can make in an affluent society (and there simply aren't affluent societies in any other system) are often portrayed as destructive and soul-deadening in the media and in many of our learning institutions.

Competitive kids are encouraged to compete against other kids in organized games or are urged to get better marks in schools in order to attend better schools later on. There is tremendous restless energy in all this, but little opportunity for the kids themselves to do anything on their own. Simple score keeping can become the essential measurement of a kid's life and a parent's success.

This book proceeds from several fundamentally different points:

- That kids can think for themselves at a very early age,
- That the market ethic of fair exchange is a better path to self-esteem than all the social theories that teach self-sacrifice and obedience to authority, and
- That doing useful work at an early age is good for young poets and scientists as well as for young entrepreneurs.

Families themselves reflect the prejudices of the times.

One family will blame society for everything; themselves and their kids for nothing. They will never know self-respect because they will never admit self-responsibility.

Another family will find parents pitted bitterly against kids; kids voraciously, even violently exploiting parents. Feeling powerless against everyone else, they will take out all of their aggressions against one another.

In one family, without a book in the house, learning any skill or even to read, may seem a useless affectation. In another, every book, every magazine, every lesson may be solely instrumental, aimed at some definition of employability, of how to get along, be popular, be fashionable, be usable.

And then there is this kind of family: Development of the mind is prized for its own sake, the human mind being regarded as the supreme instrument of human action, the agency of human creativity, the definer and author of human progress. Work is prized as the process through which human minds react with the environment and transform parts of it to human purposes. Work, which includes the generation of ideas as well as the manipulation of materials, is viewed as the legitimate source of wealth.

Wealth, which can be money, reputation, self-satisfaction, honors, or whatever else of value, is important to the producer as the legitimate, accumulated profit from successful transactions in the market. This is as true of a "poor" poet with a rich reputation among members of a comparatively small market as it is for a great merchandiser with a market of millions.

Some parents hope to shield their children from what they regard as the harsh realities of the marketplace. They teach them that it is more blessed to give than receive. They neglect to teach them that what a successful free marketer does is just that: He or she gives what buyers want. That is a precise definition of success in the market. No matter the motive of the seller, whether it's the sheerest, coldest greed or whatever, the fact is that there can't be a successful transaction unless they are prepared to offer something that someone else wants badly enough to buy.

Some parents, angry at some part of the market or some practitioner in it, teach that profit is an unworthy motive and that only "the people" or their representatives are selfless enough to do good things. They neglect the common sense appreciation that "the people" exist only as a meaningless abstraction until they make choices in a marketplace of some sort—political or commercial. They neglect the common sense appreciation that even politics is a marketplace but with a chilling addition: Those with political power can use guns to enforce *their* decisions. They are historically less restrained than merchants and manufacturers who must rely on persuasion.

Every family faces this matter of profits in one way or another. So do their kids. Just ignoring it as not worthy of family discussion won't make it go away. Kids will still wonder what parents do for a living. They will certainly be curious about how much disposable income is available. And yet, kids who may be taught the terms and sensibilities of sexuality as early as they exhibit any curiosity, who may be encouraged to know every convolution of a family's genealogy, may be abruptly halted when asking about family finances.

Money, the market, profit, work, wealth are shoved aside like unwelcome relatives so that childish innocence may be protected. A child who is encouraged to know about the birds and the bees but who is censored from knowing anything of the economic life and responsibilities of a family is most likely to treat sex as a recreation without consequences and to view participation in a family as a game of forever getting with no reason to give.

Ignorance of work and wealth is a deadly ignorance.

Whiny, pampered, rude kids, the sort you hate to

have in your house when their parents visit, have not experienced the disciplines of the free market. Their product, which may be only their personality, has not been subjected to any exchange agreement at all. No matter what they do—the eager parents buy it. You are expected to be as careless a consumer. You may pay the price to keep the parents as friends. But what you'd love to do, admit it, is to simply turn down the kids' obnoxious bargain, tell them their wild, whiny wares aren't wanted, and have them wait outside or in a corner. There is a powerful signal in such market decisions.

Kids who understand the give and take of a market economy and who start that understanding by being a participating part of the entire economy of the family— including its social economy—are more likely to be careful and cooperative when they visit you. They will understand that things broken must be replaced, that the toys of others—including adults—are as important as their own and that a visit is not an invitation to an invasion.

What you, as a parent or as someone else with influence on a young person, can do to enhance a youngster's early understanding of exchanges, individual responsibility, the necessities of choice, and the creation of wealth, may be the only early experience a young person will have with the world of real economics. Without that experience, they could easily grow up in what could be called an intellectual and ethical underclass, easy prey to fashions, fads, and political preachments, and unsure of their own ability to make choices that matter.

Life is not, as you probably know, a series of random social collisions. You are not powerless to make choices, no matter where you are or who you are: rich, poor, greatly gifted or not, physically strong or weak. Not everyone in the meanest, poorest neighborhood behaves the same way. Some choose to retain dignity and self-esteem, to work hard, move out, and move up. Others do not. It is not society that has decided. It is they who have decided.

This book is for young people who may take to heart that essential notion; they are free to choose many things, to go many ways, and they are primarily responsible for the choices. Some will acquire this book on their own, thus making a choice on their own. Others may be given the book by someone like yourself. The young person will still have to decide whether to pay any attention to it or not—and even those who choose to ignore its every page, but do so because it has caused them to think about it all and come to their own conclusions, will be made stronger, at least, by having done the thinking and made the decision.

The best result of all, for my money, would be that young persons take the information in the book, decide whether it is valid or not, and then, after adding personal observations, take off independently enterprising on their own.

Realistically, though, most will seek some help from an older person.

And what can the older person provide? Experience, of course. Some investment capital, if needed. But mainly encouragement of the young person's ability to think creatively and independently, and to understand the vital difference between merely having a job and having a future.

Look at it this way if you happen to be dealing with a teenager. There are plenty of opportunities for jobs for teens; fast food places are now paying up to $5.75 an hour in affluent suburbs, while paying minimum wage in inner cities. A pizza parlor in suburban Atlanta offers $7.00 an hour for teen workers. That's $280 for a 40-hour week, more than a beginning reporter on a small daily paper can make even with a college degree in journalism.

Kids from very poor families may have to seek such work, even at minimum wage, just to survive, and help their family to survive. Kids from more affluent families may take on such jobs just to pile up some money.

But, in either case, an older, more experienced person could help them appreciate the difference between that work as an end in itself and as a tough step toward a better future.

Even the poorest kid will face some choices about the money earned. Every cent spent on fashionable clothes represents a choice not to save the money for something else—education, books, tools.

The same sort of choices will face the more affluent kids; they can be applauded for spending it all on clothes or recordings—with parents often boasting that their kids "earn their own" even if they promptly throw it all away. Or... they can be encouraged to do exactly what a prudent poor kid will do—save some for investment in the future.

Fine for teenagers, but what about really little kids? How can they begin to understand the meaning of work and wealth and responsibility?

One way is to put the child on a salary as soon as possible, turning over a certain amount of money each week in return for doing a few chores around the house. But it shouldn't stop there. By the time a child is going to a regular school there should be some connection between the salary, between chores and responsibility, and the real, outside world. Making the child responsible for the purchase of basic school supplies—from the child's own salary—is one way to do it.

To make it even more realistic, the child might also be made responsible for paying for some minor item of clothing such as socks. The salary, of course, should be adequate to make the purchases possible plus leaving some over for wholly discretionary use—or saving. But think of what an important lesson is learned when a child has to buy a pair of socks! They are less likely, at the very least, to treat them as disposable, minor items. The parent, on the other hand, must be prepared for some sharp differences in taste when it comes to what kind of socks the child will buy. Some 10-year-olds might even be trusted to shop for groceries on their way home from school, as a paid chore and as a splendid way to learn about the value of nourishment that easily could be taken for granted.

In every instance like this, the major lesson being made familiar is that the world is one of daily, incessant choices; that people can and do make the choices; that they are responsible for the choices. All of life involves choosing between alternatives. The more conscious a child can be of choice and responsibility at any level— from the mundane purchase of groceries to the sometimes shattering decisions about friends, about interests, about how to spend time—the better.

As the child grows, and his salary goes up, along with chores, a few other items of necessity might be added to the list of things for which the child is responsible: underclothing, tee shirts; then more serious purchases such as shoes when the child is in the fourth or fifth grade. If kids make terrible buys, or actually ruin some item of clothing through no fault of their own, a parent can either practice charity—making sure that the child understands what that is, or practice some informal banking by lending the child enough money to make up for the loss—but charging some interest in the process.

By high school, a salaried child should be very comfortable with long range planning, careful buying, taking care of what is bought, and not wasting resources of any sort.

Will that make the kid a sourpuss or prematurely old? Why should it? Kids who are brought up on fresh fruit rather than candy sweets seem to enjoy a decent childhood—and better health. Why should a kid who is fed candied notions of money and responsibility have a richer childhood than one who learns early on that they are respected enough by older people to *have* responsibilities, to be trusted, and to make choices on their own.

Elizabeth Crow, editor-in-chief of *Parents Magazine*, wrote about how her children were playing in the garage and turned the bicycle-wheeled garden cart into a sort of rickshaw, and asked Mom and Dad if they would pay for rides.

"At first, I worried that this entrepreneurial spirit just meant that they'd become horrible little money-grubbers. Then I worried that the children were taking unfair advantage of our friends and relatives. And perhaps they were. But the cart-ride company also fulfilled a real need for Sam and Rachel: It supplemented their meager allowances in time for Christmas shopping. And, these days, there aren't that many ways for an eight-year-old and a five-year-old to make money...

"So, we've decided that, within reason, the children can invent their own businesses. As long as they're cooperating and delivering on their promises, they can sell as many rides or do as many chores as the market will permit..."

Actually, the problem with the proposal for a salaried child, or any other idea in this book, probably won't be with the kids themselves. Kids, if given a chance early enough, seem universally eager to try new things, to strike out on their own, to be ingenious and adventurous. Parents can be the problem. Some parents simply don't like children. They have them by accident or in keeping with social fashion. But they don't like them. The kids of such parents could benefit mightily by striking out on their own as soon as possible and the friend or relative who helps may be a friend indeed—and in need.

There are parents who are just too busy to work with their children. Busy parents should appreciate busy, self-reliant children; and the children, in turn, may understand their parents better as they themselves become busier—and richer!

Other parents may care mainly about what the neighbors think. They'll opt for whatever is fashionable and then subject their kids to it. Of all the sorts of parents a kid can be stuck with, that sort is probably the most unnerving, morally and creatively debilitating, and wasteful of the wonderful years of bursting, young energy. Good luck to the children who have to deal with such parents, who will have to, on their own, become real people and not just pleasure puppets being jerked around by "doting" parents.

For the parent who sees the wonder in the little kid in the house, or for the older friend who wants to help a kid, the grandest gift will be to encourage a sense of self-worth and of enterprise and to nurture early interests whether in selling, science, engineering, computing, the arts or whatever.

The matter of interest is crucial. This is not a book

to recommend that the only impulse to nurture in a young person is the specific impulse to make money. Some people have the making of money as their only goal. It's their grand game. Most people have as their first object doing something that excites them, that interests and engrosses them, that focuses them, centers them. People who do things well usually *do* well. A person wanting only to make money, not even excited by the gaming of it, but simply fixed on acquisition, seems more a study in eccentricity and often in frustrated, eventual failure.

The purpose of a free market emphasis in a child's early life is not to focus them solely on marketing but is, rather, to give whatever truly interests the child a material, reality-measured dimension.

Does this mean to preclude dreaming, the wildest fantasies of a young mind? Not at all. But wouldn't the child dreaming of roaming between the stars be strengthened, not weakened, by knowing that the trip will take material as well as intellectual accomplishment?

Some rare children may do nothing but dream, and whether this is sheer escape from the world around them or just the wondrous prelude to a life of invention is a judgement call. And yet, even for such a child, it is hard to imagine that a chore or two or a straightforward participation in the economic life of the family could be harmful.

David Packard, co-founder of the trailblazing electronic firm of Hewlett-Packard, in a letter to the author, commenting on the proposal for this book, objected to an emphasis on making money. He wrote that "I became interested in engineering at a very early age, was intrigued by the existing developments in technology, and I started the company because I wanted to do something in a technical field. I was not at all motivated by wanting to be

a capitalist, or even with the hope of making a lot of money."

The suggestion is not to be overlooked. Wanting to do the work that pleases you can be the most powerful motivation of all. Being in business may be the best way to assure the possibility of doing it. Being in a successful business may be the best way to assure being able to continue to do it. And, of course, whether the greatly talented David Packard wanted to be a capitalist or not is beside the point. He was, and is, one. And we are all a bit better off *because* he is!

Today's parents and today's children have an obvious barrier between them. The parents come from yesterday while the children are tomorrow. Although it is bound to make many a parent grit their teeth, it should be always kept in mind that what was conventional in our past, as parents, may seem almost grotesque to young people. Patience all around is called for.

According to management experts interviewed by *Business Week* magazine, these are some broad differences between today's and tomorrow's executives that could correspond as well to the children who will become those executives and the parents who nurture them:

The Old Generation	*The New Generation*
Cautious	Eager to take risks
Insecure	Optimistic
Resistant to change	Flexible
Loyal to company	Willing to job-hop
Value job security	Want to make impact
Male	Male or female
White	Ethnically diverse
A good day's work	Workaholic
Comfortable in bureaucracies	Crave autonomy, power
Conservative Republican	Independent

The Old Generation	*The New Generation*
People-oriented	Numbers-oriented
Slide-rules, legal pads	Computers, data networks
College degree	Advanced degree
25-year career plan	Instant gratification

Selling children short seems to be the dedication of our education today. Nowhere is this more apparent than in regard to economics.

In "The Contribution of Elementary and Middle Schools to Education for Business" (University of Colorado), Lawrence Senesh wrote that:

"Our boys and girls are growing up with scarcely any idea of the structure and functioning of the American economic system; consequently, as adults they shy away from everything that deals with economic topics in newspapers and magazines. This economic illiteracy largely stems from the preconceptions many educators have concerning the learning abilities of our children. They say that elementary school children are not ready to comprehend economic concepts, but experiments in Elkhart, Indiana, have shown that the fundamental theories of economics and of other areas in the social sciences can be meaningfully related to children's everyday experiences.

"Many primary school teachers think that economic theories have little place in the elementary school curriculum because the children have not yet acquired skills in reading, writing, and arithmetic. These arguments have little validity...

"In the primary grades in many schools, for instance, children are taken to banks and shown the vaults. They 'discover' that the purpose of banks is safekeeping money. This 'discovery' is untrue since the main purpose of banks is granting credit, a concept not mentioned in primary grades. Primary school children are also introduced to the operation of a grocery store. Teachers build counters. Children bring canned goods from home to stock their grocery shelves. This activity usually centers around teaching the skill for making change. There is no reference to competition, profit, risk, or loss, characteristics of the business system..."

Little wonder then, as Larry Reynolds, president of Small Business Advisory, a Washington-based information company, has written:

"By the time we become adults, most of us have learned to look at the world only as others see it. Entrepreneurs and artists are different in that they can look at the same thing we all do and still think something different...

"What makes entrepreneurs able to tackle that most difficult thing? They have the courage, heart and drive to make their visions a reality...

"True entrepreneurs look at the world with what Zenas Block, of New York University's Center For Entrepreneurial Studies, calls 'creative dissatisfaction.' There is not a thing on the planet that cannot be done better...

"Innovation is not limited to some kind of invention or breakthrough technology. It can also be a new process or different way of doing business. Maybe something as simple as new markets for old products...

"It is better to outthink your competition than to outspend them, especially if you do not have very deep pockets to begin with...

"What is exciting is that we are surrounded by entrepreneurial opportunities that we can see, provided we choose to see them. The trick is to pay attention to your small ideas, then see if they can be turned into bigger ones...

"It all starts with daring to think something different."

Luther H. Hodges, a former United States Secretary of Commerce, puts it this way:

"If ignorance paid dividends, most Americans could make a fortune out of what they don't know about economics...

"Wherever we look, some of the most important events are economic. All of us are affected by recessions, by unemployment, by inflation...

"Individuals have to answer these questions for themselves in a democracy; we don't want dictatorial men to make decisions for us...

"No more than 10 to 15 percent of today's high-school students...will ever take a separate course in economics, either in high school or in college...

"Many think you can push up standards simply by raising wages or increasing Government spending...

"Economics teaches us that we must constantly choose between alternatives...If we spend, we can't save; if we buy this, we can't buy that; the more taxes we impose to pay for Government services, the less money there is for private spending...

"[*Economics*] equips us for orderly thinking about our resources...

"For years farsighted professional, civic, business and labor organizations have sought to encourage better economic education. We need more of this organized effort."

The truth of the matter, however, is that the main burden of getting a youngster to think about economics as something important, real, and lively is going to have to be a family project, not a school one. And it will take patience, as an article in *U.S. News and World Report* pointed out:

"Most parents only talk about money when there are problems, when they are yelling and screaming.

"In conveying attitudes about money to children, it's best to start early. By age three or four, children understand that money buys things and are capable of selecting a small item in a store...and paying for it."

The child, not the parent, should pay for the purchase. An allowance is the "primary money-management tool for children," according to family finance specialist Patricia Tengel, of the University of Maryland.

By five or six, a child should have some walking around money under his control. By college age, a youngster should be able to budget for a semester or even a whole school year.

When an allowance is spent, extra cash for a bailout should not be simply granted. As mentioned earlier, a loan might be appropriate—and instructive. It might also be useful to give a kid a special job to do for extra pay in an emergency.

Tom Taylor in his book *Kids and Cash*, says "Parents don't owe their children a college education, or cars, or trips to Europe. We owe them self-reliance."

Early years in compulsory schools, despite the best intentions of parents, can discourage rather than encourage that sense of self and of self-reliance. The question has become crucial, as a matter of fact.

A parent interested in a young person's attitude toward creativity and freedom simply has to be concerned about the way things are going in education generally.

Today there is virtually an underground war going on in American education. Although it is rarely mentioned publicly, it is a struggle upon which will depend the future character of the country, its productive systems, its standard of living, the civility of its cities, science, technology, health care, and fiscal integrity. It will even determine the nature or existence of tax-supported, government education. It certainly will have a lot to do with how the young people in whom you are interested will be equipped to make a future for themselves.

The struggle is simply stated. One side holds that the purpose of education, public or otherwise, is to teach facts so that pupils may acquire specific skills and later become employable. This is known as content teaching. The other side holds that the purpose of education is to encourage independent reasoning power so that data may be understood, not just memorized. This is known as process teaching.

As the struggle is now waged, it is an either-or battle. Schools go one way or the other. It is, in effect, academic war to the death. If, as the author strongly recommends, you consider the importance of process teaching for a young person who wants to be self-reliant and engage in creative free market enterprises, you should familiarize yourself with the struggle and think how you can assure some process teaching for the young people in whom you are interested—no matter the offering of formal educators in your area.

And who takes which side? Is there a clear liberal-conservative, or Democrat-Republican split? Is there a clear moral or religious position? Is there a class angle to it? How are schools themselves split by it?

In general, liberals and conservatives, Democrats

and Republicans, are moving strongly, and together, toward the side of content teaching. They have different reasons but a similar supportive direction.

Conservatives like content teaching because it reinforces habits of obedience to traditional values. Liberals, although not wildly enthusiastic about content teaching, by and large support it because they have special reasons to oppose process teaching. Many of them consider process teaching to be elitist and to encourage the advancement of individual students rather than serving the favorite liberal purpose of education which is to make all students equal. Liberals and conservatives both seem to equate content teaching with the increasingly popular notion of "getting back to basics." Conservatives like the back to basics movement because they assume it will include discipline, obedience, and order. Liberals like it because they feel it offers the best chance for the employment of minorities and also because it is virtually "teacher proof," and thus fits the egalitarian idea of mass production teachers. (Process teaching, on the other hand, reinforces the recognition of outstanding teachers and also emphasizes the importance of individual teacher talent and performance.)

The usual definition of getting back to basics is a demand for rote drill in reading, the multiplication table, and the sequence of historic events. Process teaching actually is even more basic. Its emphasis on reading is so sharp that children are encouraged *in all grades* to read at their own pace rather than risk the frustrations of having to conform to some average pace.

A single failure of content teaching is that bright students often are completely turned off from reading by having to wait for slower classmates, while the slower ones, if they ever fall behind, just give up on reading entirely.

Studies of adult illiterates strongly suggest that their problems began in the very early grades. In content teaching, an illiterate child can "get away with it" by memorizing texts and getting lucky on multiple choice tests. In process teaching they have to understand what they read and be able to read unfamiliar texts. Similarly, in math skills, process teaching emphasizes understanding of how the processes work and their applications to real-world problems. Process teaching, in effect, adds Reasoning to the traditional three R's. Content teaching not only ignores reasoning but actively discourages it in favor of "teaching to the test."

(A special aside regarding the so-called New Math: Parents have, for sensible reasons, come to equate the New Math with a dangerous ignoring of ordinary computational skills. New Math, actually, should never have been taught as math at all, but as logic—which it largely encompasses. Logic is, in fact, crucial to the reasoning mind. With it, the ordinary computational skills become "understandable" rather than just memorized. In process teaching, logic, computational skills, and reasoning all flow together. Process teaching is, actually, far more classical than any modern fads. It harks back to the medieval schools in which logic, observation, and reasoned arguments formed the basis of an education from which any future goals or tasks could be addressed effectively and flexibly.)

Many religious groups take the position not only to support content teaching but to strongly denounce and demand an end to process teaching. Process teaching, which calls for pupils to think for themselves to the extent practicable, is felt by fundamentalists to encourage the questioning of authority and to emphasize human intelligence as opposed to divine guidance. Between the liberal opposition to process teaching as elitist and the fundamentalist opposition to it as encouraging nonconformist thought, there has been little space to achieve a sensible compromise between the two contending positions.

There is a very strong class angle to the struggle. Middle and upper-class homes in which there is a built-in respect for learning, lots of books, limited TV viewing, a home computer, family discussions, encouragement of individual responsibility, already are involved in a sort of process education—at home. Also, many such families send their children to private secular schools where they can expect an emphasis on process teaching. Some of these families even keep their children home, for home schooling, where process teaching is overwhelmingly popular. (On the other hand, of course, fundamentalist families may prefer *private* religious schools because they *reject* process teaching.)

Poor families and even middle-class families, where there is a constant struggle just to get by, where there is no particular interest in creativity or independent thinking, want specific skills for their kids. They want them to get jobs, to be employees, not to take risks as entrepreneurs and innovators. Their children are the backbone of the widely publicized banality of students today, the kids who say that all they want is a car, a job, snazzy clothes, and early retirement.

In schools themselves, young, eager, and enthusiastic teachers are likely to want to teach process, to engage their pupils, even in the earliest grades, in the process of thinking rather than the process of memorizing facts, or content. Older teachers may prefer the order and predictability of content teaching.

Administrators, by and large, favor content teaching because so many parents approve of it and find it reassuringly familiar, because it is easily quantifiable for record keeping, and because they wish to avoid any hint of favoring bright pupils—a favoritism that is almost guaranteed to bring howls of outrage from the professional representatives of the disadvantaged. (The disadvantaged, for the purposes of government education, never include bright, energetic students denied a chance to move at their own speed and for their own purposes.)

But what difference does it make?

In Politics:

As most people now recognize, liberals and conservatives have become nothing but organizational opponents with no significant differences. An obvious alternative, with profound free market meaning, would be a doctrine of absolute personal responsibility, consensual agreement, and non-aggression. This is the politics or, better, ethic of people able to think independently, reason in regard to consequences, and plan for their own futures. Process teaching supports the emergence of such people. Content teaching, emphasizing authority and regimentation, discourages it.

Or look at it this way: The Declaration of Independence is a "process" oriented document. It says that the individual is sovereign, must think independently, and support government only as a means to that end. The Constitution, on the other hand, has evolved as a "content" document in which the power of the federal government has become supreme, in which even the meaning of the

Constitution is derived from federal authority (the Supreme Court), and in which independence of thought, enterprise, and property is regularly sacrificed to the collectivist "needs of society" (again as defined by federal authority).

In the spirit of this content sort of politics, the old slogan of "my country, right or wrong" has become simplified to "my President, right or wrong" or even "my Party, right or wrong." Similarly, the concept of citizenship has deteriorated from Jefferson's "sturdy yeomanry" of free and independent thinkers to the modern concept of being merely a voter, one who selects someone to be, in effect, a surrogate citizen, to debate issues and to make decisions.

The New England Town Meetings were a good example of politics as a process, demanding participation. Millions of people glued to their TV sets, choosing candidates on the basis of their dramatic performances, is politics in the "content" sense just as teaching American history as simply a drill exercise of dates and names is content education compared to the "process" approach which would actively engage students in the immediate politics of their own social and civic settings.

In Productivity:

The days when a good employee was simply one who followed rules, was loyal to the company, and didn't make waves, are fast ending. There is still a demand for that type, of course. But the most rapidly growing demand is for people who will take responsibility, actively contribute to production processes, not have to be told every moment what to do, and accept personal responsibility.

The more advanced and flexible our technology becomes, the more demand there will be for such people. Put it another way: The better our machines become, the more need for human beings to excel at what the machines can't yet do: reason, imagine, create, invent, innovate.

The dramatic decline of labor unions in this country is just one very visible symptom of this change in the way we work; the change from regimented to reasoning workers.

The more process teaching there is in the country, the more reasoning people there will be available to use the technology, not to mention invent and innovate it!

The present plight of steel and autoworkers is a tribute to content teaching in every sense. These were workers who, in their education, acquired rote and specific skills, became used to high wages for the repetitive performance of those skills in highly unionized situations, and then were left high and dry when their services were no longer needed or were priced out of the market.

They can honestly complain that they never were equipped to do anything but work in the specific factories of their childhoods. They weren't. Flexible thinking, adaptation to new ideas, reasoning in order to learn new things were never part of their schooling. Ability to think their way through new situations was never encouraged. It probably was discouraged.

They were taught that if you just passed the multiple-choice tests, didn't cause trouble, and got out with a high school diploma (even if only able to read at a third grade level) that everything would be fine. And, for a long time, it was. Now it isn't. These people, late in life, now must become students again, learning new skills, probably relocating, starting all over again—or remain where they are, stuck in despair and welfare. Process teaching would have prepared them for change. Content teaching taught them "facts" which they now can't use and whose value has shrunk to zero.

Virtually all children now exposed only to content teaching, to multiple-choice testing, and to rote achievement will be doomed to being part of a permanent underclass of low wage, drudge labor—and the market even for that will shrink steadily given the existence of minimum wage laws and the relative advantages of buying a good machine to do mindless work.

In Science and Technology:

The most dramatic differences show up here. Science is the most pure form of process thinking. It is based on curiosity, a questioning of all things, a search for data and for the *meaning* of the data (not just the recognition of it), a demand for independent verification, a respect for logic, a consideration of consequences—and leaps of intuition beyond apparent reason. Science is, in short, everything that content teaching abhors (skeptical, freewheeling, anti-authoritarian, non-dogmatic, partly intuitive, rigorous in demands for proof, doggedly logical, and supremely confident of human ability). Science is, in short, just what process teaching encourages.

Advances in the material applications of scientific propositions (there are no facts in science, only propositions or theories), which we call technology, also involve unbounded imagination, risk-taking, rule-breaking, and independent thought. That's the stuff of process thinking.

Most of the technological innovations of this century have come in small research or commercial operations where independent thinking can be encouraged.

Large companies have been notoriously slow to even adopt, much less invent, new technologies. And these same companies, growing to sizes and styles that more or less duplicate governmental bureaucracies, have given rise to the major markets for content-taught employees— dull, obedient, safe.

It is notable that the newer breed of executive, such as the high-rolling, high-tech, risk-taking Ross Perot, has tangled dramatically with the old industrial bureaucracies to exemplify the difference between process thinking and content thinking. General Motors, after buying Perot's electronic data processing company for enough to make him the company's largest single shareholder, then paid him more than $700 million to buy up his stock and get him off the board of directors where he had steadily opposed executive featherbedding, complacency, and what he called "the bean counting" mentality of people who want always to do things by the book—the way content teaching does!

Science always has depended upon maverick minds. Process teaching can encourage such minds but probably can't produce them. And, probably, content teaching can't suppress them. But that's thinking in the genius range. Schools aren't for geniuses anyway. They are for the other people who expand the frontiers of science even if they don't breach them. Process teaching can encourage them. Content teaching probably would frustrate them.

Technology depends upon a broader range of people, on entrepreneurs who see a need, on engineers who see a way, on inventors who see something new, on the great industrial innovators — all of whom seem to be more process oriented than "fact" or content oriented. The future of our technology, then, will be crucially impacted by the growth or suppression of process teaching.

In World Affairs:

Already, the striking difference between content teaching and process teaching is causing concern in places as different as the Soviet Union and Japan. Both countries have placed a heavy emphasis on conformity—communists by brute force, the Japanese by tradition. Both face significant choices—just as we do—in continuing to support almost exclusively content teaching or running the immense risks of social change through allowing process teaching to take its place.

Process thinking in Japan is best exemplified by the garage-mechanic turned entrepreneur, Soichiro Honda. Content thinking is best exemplified by the highly publicized Ministry of Trade and Industry (MITI) which once actively discouraged Honda's small-car dreams and which, for all its publicity, is now seen as a bureaucratic drag on Japanese enterprise, encouraging sure things, and discouraging imaginative, risky new ideas.

In Japanese schools, however, there is some room for process teaching—but only for the best-connected students. Everyone else is subjected to a drill and rote, march and memorize education whose creativity-curbing slogan is "the nail that sticks up, must be hammered down."

Should Japanese policymakers decide to encourage more and more process teaching, the society will reap great benefits in innovation and in people able to think for and take care of themselves—but the society also will reap the inevitable whirlwind of social change that such a break from a conformist society implies. The notion of no gain without pain certainly applies here.

The Soviet Union faces the toughest choice of all. If its policymakers encourage more independence of thought, they will encourage the abolition of the very authoritarian system through which they have risen to power. Ordinarily there probably would be no question that the leaders would opt for anything but continued authority and the sort of content-based education that supports it.

Today there is a new element. In order to become a relatively self-sufficient industrial, not to mention agricultural, society (a goal that has eluded the communists for more than a half century of promises and tyranny), the Soviet Union is going to have to permit the dissemination of such tools of modern industry as the personal computer. With the information disseminating capabilities of these computers, the oppressive secrecy upon which all tyranny eventually rests will have to teeter.

Already, just the introduction of modern photocopying machines into the Soviet Union has opened up vast new streams of dissident information exchange which the rulers have been unable to dam. In other parts of the communist empire even such devices as typewriters are recognized as inherently anti-authoritarian and are heavily licensed and controlled. Can such societies be full participants in what is happening in this latter part of the Twentieth Century? Of course not. They must change or decay.

In Culture:

It is important to realize that the role of schools in providing us with a homogeneous culture and morality died some time ago and simply cannot be revived no matter how earnestly many conservatives and religious fundamentalists wish it could.

The *national* culture of this land is now established by, disseminated by, and controlled by television and not by the schools, politics, churches, or any other institutions.

This is not to say that there is not important room left for local and special cultures or that other institutions cannot influence TV.

Advertisers can, of course, influence it, but not much. As long as there is far more demand for ad space on TV than there is space itself, the influence of any one advertiser will be slight. The threat to withdraw from TV advertising is not taken seriously by those who enjoy a virtual monopoly of the air waves thanks to government licensing of them.

But even if the monopoly were broken and a free market developed in television—as it could even now with the proliferation of cable, if cable itself can break loose from government licensing—the schools still would not be important national cultural forces.

The national culture would remain electronic, even if somewhat more enriched or varied than it is today.

To blame the schools for children who accept violence easily, who judge their own, and everyone else's, worth by what they can buy rather than what they can do, whose attention spans are slight, and whose energy levels are those of couch potatoes, is simply to look in the wrong place. Only TV provides the endless images that are *the culture*.

In Morality and Values:
It is in this very area that conservatives and liberals have most muddied the waters while religious fundamentalists have whipped them into a virtual whirlpool.

Take the family. In the 1980's a President who is himself the participant in a modern family (i.e. divorced, scattered kids, working parents) kept talking about traditional families. Few exist, not even in politics. Most marriages lead to divorce. Most women work. Most of these same women, despite Biblical commands of subordination, simply are not being subordinated.

Schools committed to teaching the values of traditional family life might have an impact in isolated areas. And, certainly, in a free society, the opportunity to have such schools should be absolute. But TV, the national culture, will do more to determine the actual family culture for most Americans. The behavior of prominent people, also, will have a powerful effect on the way people will want to live. Government schools can, of course, tilt toward any value or morality that bureaucrats in power want. But changes in the bureaucracy of the schools is as slow as in any other bureaucracy and, given the constant change of political fashion, there is an inclination for schools simply to coast along, doing the same things as long as possible, rather than risking change.

Conservatives have long felt that simply introducing prayer into the government school system would set everything right. Why should they think that this particular expansion or exercise of government power would be any more desirable or effective than any other sort of government intervention? Yet, the issue of school prayer has become virtually the entire issue of conservative interest in the government's school system.

Liberals, on the other hand, have encouraged every effort to turn the schools into effective support groups for other forms of government intervention—mainly the regulatory intervention of government into commerce and industry. Just as conservatives put their faith in prayer in the government schools, the liberals put their faith in consumer protection in the government schools. Let anyone suggest that religion is an option in a free society and conservatives stoutly argue that this is a Christian nation. Let anyone argue that capitalism (another option in a free society) works best when left alone and liberals stoutly argue that this is the law of the jungle.

Fundamentalists take the conservative view about school prayer, but go considerably beyond it. Just as liberals go to ridiculous lengths to prohibit *any* discussion of religion in the schools (as, for instance, not wanting it recalled that the early settlers often were driven by a quest for religious freedom), so do fundamentalists go to extraordinary lengths to oppose any discussion of the scientific *method* in schools. The well-known opposition to teaching the *theory* of evolution is minor in its implication compared to some of the other fundamentalist objections revealed in the recent court case (Mozert vs. Hawkins, in Tennessee) involving parental objection to science in the classroom.

Among the specific objections were "relying on common sense," the notion that "you can do anything if you try hard," and "overuse of the imagination." If parents want to withhold such teaching from their children, it should be of little concern to the rest of us. There probably always will be some useful work that can be done by people who do not use their imagination very much, who don't believe they are capable of doing many things, and who don't exercise common sense but instead go by someone else's book. In a decent future, such people would be on their own and could not expect welfare support from the rest of the population. The same should apply to any people who deliberately cut themselves off from the scientific method, technology, innovation, and enterprise. Like religion, such things should not be mandatory in a free society where people would be responsible for their own choices and the lives to which those choices lead.

• • •

Some broad conclusions and recommendations:

If your own children are involved, and assuming you want them to take full advantage of a future of rapidly changing technologies and markets, remember that the example set at home (respect for learning, logic, reason, and self-responsibility) is more important than *any* school. Reading aloud to pre-literate children probably does more to assure literacy than *any* school program. Chores, chances to earn real money for real work, will do more to instill an interest in and respect for the free market than *any* school program. In short, what you do at home is more important than what "they" do.

If your business interest depends upon brawn workers rather than brain workers, you may favor content teaching but you should do so with the recognition that it entails some externality costs such as a fair number of illiterates and an attendant higher crime rate.

If your future seems to depend more on brain workers, then process teaching is the clear choice.

If your concern is over declining moral standards, violence, juvenile delinquency, and general irresponsibility, don't look to the schools for a solution at all. Only TV can be seen, these days, as a truly national shaper of such attitudes. Breaking the federal and other licensing restrictions on TV is, thus, a more important means than changing schools to add new dimensions to national moral and ethical standards. A free market in TV could mean at least competing ideas to break present cultural homogeneity.

The same situation applies to the school system. As long as it is largely a government monopoly, its administrators will reflect government attitudes. The most gifted teachers, today, are being discouraged by the constant growth of administrative staffs and demands and the declining attention to classroom activity. The schools accurately reflect the same sort of growth in the federal government. Any legislative changes that encourage private schools and home schooling will help break the monopoly that government schools now enjoy over a crucial aspect of our very future.

Perhaps the most radical proposal ever made along those lines has come from MIT's Seymour Papert who developed the computer language LOGO for very young children. In an eye and mind-opening book called *Mindstorms: Children, Computers and Powerful Ideas* (Basic Books, 1980), he argues that a personal computer being made available to a child may provide a more productive learning atmosphere than any formal classroom.

His book includes this truly revolutionary view which may be the most provocative statement made in our time about education, the free market, and individualism:

"Increasingly, [*computers*] will be the private property of individuals, and this will gradually return to the individual the power to determine patterns of education. Education will become more of a private act, and people with good ideas, different ideas, exciting ideas will no longer be faced with a dilemma where they either have to 'sell' their ideas to a conservative bureaucracy or shelve them. They will be able to offer them in an open marketplace directly to consumers. There will be new opportunities for imagination and originality. There might be a renaissance of thinking about education."

Less radical, but impressively practical, is the work of the Institute for the Advancement of Philosophy for Children, at Montclair State College, Upper Montclair, New Jersey. Its teaching materials — rigorously emphasizing analysis, reason, logic, and intellectual self-responsibility — are being used in several hundred elementary schools already. The results are striking: Pupils are uniformly advanced in their ability to think and learn. They face one handicap. On standardized tests they are likely to be slower than others because they tend to grapple for real understanding of the questions, even argue with their meanings, and thus take longer to think it all over. For anyone interested in seeing process teaching material at its very best, the catalog of this remarkable institute offers great opportunities.

Finally, if you find, in a local school, teachers who are interested in bucking the system and giving children a chance to think, do what you can to support them. They are a golden asset. Remember, the true basics are the four, not three, R's—Readin', 'Riting, 'Rithmetic AND REASON.

At the heart of everything this book has been about is the value of the reasoning mind. Without its development, a young person is prey to every passing fad and whim of popular culture, including the current one that insists on keeping young people out of the marketplace for as long as possible.

With the development of a reasoning mind, everything in this book is open and possible for any young person. Without it, the world must seem a cold and closed system with joyless jobs as the only future. With the development of the young mind and the unleashing of the young imagination and youthful energy, the future seems exciting again—bright and hopeful.

13

DIRECTORY

The following directory of organizations and publications is offered as a starting place for those interested in finding out more about entrepreneurial activities. It is certainly not a complete listing of all groups offering information in this area, but it is a list we feel at least touches most of the topics discussed in this book. We encourage you to dig out other sources on your own.

ACE (UK)
Business Studies Department
University of Stirling
Stirling FK9 4LA
England

ACE (UK) is the British branch of an international network, Association of Collegiate Entrepreneurs, which brings "together the resources and information of the world's young entrepreneurs." The group is based largely within the circles of higher education, but membership is open to all.

American Association of Black Women Entrepreneurs
1326 Missouri Avenue
Suite 4
Washington, DC 20011
202-231-3751

The Association's objectives are to "unite black women entrepreneurs; encourage business ownership as a career option; encourage joint ventures, knowledge exchange, and fellowship;" also provides training in management, credit and capital formation, and marketing.

American Association of Individual Investors
612 N. Michigan Avenue
Chicago, IL 60611
312-280-0170

The Association is for people who make their own investment decisions. They offer home-study courses on various investment topics. The group's educational programs are designed to help "develop an investment philosophy and decision making process based on individual objectives, capabilities and attitudes; evaluate the suitability of different investment vehicles; evaluate specific investment opportunities; obtain information necessary for effective decision making; and to relate various investments to each other and to the general economic climate."

American Business Women's Association
P.O. Box 8728
9100 Ward Parkway
Kansas City, MO 64114
816-361-6621

The Association attempts to improve "the professional, educational, cultural and social advancement of

Enterprise Publishing Co., Inc.
725 Market Street
Wilmington, Delaware
-19801-

Dear Sirs / Madam,
    I am interested
complete list of yo
interests include
self-help, legal
and entrepreneu

business women." Scholarships are awarded each year to women students and to women in business.

American Entrepreneurs Association
2311 Pontius Avenue
Los Angeles, CA 90064
213-478-0437

The Association is for people interested in business opportunities and starting new businesses. Disseminates information and sponsors specialized education. Publishes *Entrepreneur* magazine, which provides examples of small business opportunities and offers hints for the small businessperson. The magazine also publishes a Franchise Yearbook.

American Federation of Small Business
407 S. Dearborn Street
Chicago, IL 60605
312-427-0207

The Federation conducts educational programs, including Excellence in Education, Repeal of Bureaucratic Regulatory Agencies, and Tax Discrimination Against Small Business. The group also provides speakers on "Free Enterprise — The American Dream" and compiles statistics on small business.

Arco Publishing, Inc.
219 Park Avenue South
New York, NY 10003

Arco publishes a Career Guidance Series of books which provides kids with information about careers. The books discuss "what education background is essential, what skills are necessary, and advantages and disadvantages to each career." Books are very basic but they might give a kid information on a certain career.

Association of Collegiate Entrepreneurs
Center for Entrepreneurship
Box 147
Wichita State University
Wichita, KS 67208
316-689-3000

ACE was started in 1983 and now has chapters on most major college campuses. ACE seeks to enhance opportunities for student entrepreneurial activities through a student, faculty, and practicing entrepreneur network. ACE attempts to get entrepreneurs, venture capitalists, and consultants to act as mentors for students interested in starting entrepreneurial ventures. ACE offers students and others a vast amount of material on entrepreneurial concerns. The ACE network is extensive, so be sure to check with them if you are looking for specific information or contacts in your local area.

Association of Venture Founders
805 Third Avenue, 26th Fl.
New York, NY 10022
212-319-9220

The Association seeks "to enhance the wealth, knowledge, and business success of members." Offers educational networking for continuing education. Publishes *Venture* magazine, featuring articles on entrepreneurial opportunities, financing, computers, seed capital, business plans, franchises, and more. The magazine annually features a listing of the nation's top entrepreneurs, franchisors, and venture capitalists. A venture capital directory is also published which lists names, addresses, and phone numbers of investors.

Ben Franklin Partnerships
c/o Western PA Advanced Technology Center
4516 Henry Street
Suite 103
Pittsburgh, PA 15213
412-681-1520

Through the Partnerships, business and academic communities are working together on research projects designed to develop new technologies that have job-generating potential. The idea is to tap the high-tech expertise of the universities, share it with business professionals who can make it profitable in the marketplace, and the results are economic revitalization and a steady increase in jobs.

Black Enterprise Magazine
295 Madison Ave.
New York, NY 10017
212-889-8220

This monthly magazine covers "black economic development and business for a highly-educated, affluent, black, middle-class audience interested in business, politics, careers and international issues."

Boy Scouts of America
1325 Walnut Hill Lane
Irving, TX 75038
214-580-2000

The purpose of the BSA is to provide "educational programs for the character development, citizenship training, and mental and physical fitness of boys and young adults." The BSA offers an American Business Merit Badge and produces various publications including manuals, handbooks, and *Boys' Life* magazine.

Business Venture Network
Illini Union
1401 West Green Street
Room 299
Urbana, IL 61801
217-244-0390

Business Venture Network's goal is to "enhance and promote opportunities for students interested in entrepreneurial or intrapreneurial pursuits through the networking of students, faculty, and community entrepreneurs."

Business Week Careers
5615 West Cermack Road
Cicero, IL 60650-2290
312-656-8259

Business Week Careers is a magazine that "deals directly with the vital concerns of soon-to-be college graduates. Like choosing the right field to enter, improving interviewing skills, landing a good position with a quality employer, and surviving those first critical months on the job."

Center for Business and Economic Education
5601 West 19th Street
Lubbock, TX 79407
806-792-3221

The students at Lubbock Christian College have developed "The Chocolate Factory", a kit costing $40 which offers elementary students the opportunity to gross sales up to $80. The kit includes "two chocolate molds, five pounds of chocolate melts, sucker sticks, instructions, business forms, and other items." The kit is a packaged business program designed for young students to start their project in the classroom. Through participation in the project, kids learn production, marketing, advertising, inventory control, and profit.

Center for Entrepreneurial Management
83 Spring Street
New York, NY 10012
212-925-7304

The Center makes available published material on "developing business plans, organizing an entrepreneurial team, attracting venture capital, and obtaining patents, trademarks, and copyrights." The Center offers written material and audio cassettes addressing entrepreneurial problems. Publishes a monthly newsletter.

Center for Entrepreneurial Resources and Applied
Research
School of Continuing Education
Ball State University
Muncie, IN 47306
317-285-1588

The Center provides "consultation, basic and applied research, training, and advisory services focusing on new technology and its practical application to the problems of business, industry, and government in Indiana." The Center offers an "Entrepreneurs Guide to Venture Formation," a 42-page manual containing "a series of self-assessment exercises that enable the entrepreneur to evaluate his or her personal characteristics and business skills before embarking on the actual business plan." Cost of the Guide is $12.95.

Center for Entrepreneurship
College of Business
James Madison University
Harrisonburg, VA 22807
703-568-6726

The Center's mission is "to promote and strengthen the American entrepreneurial tradition, to enhance Virginia's economy by encouraging innovation and the creation of new enterprises, and to serve the community through education, outreach services and scholarship." The Center has sponsored a "High School Entrepreneurship Institute", and they plan to continue this program in the future. Copies of the study materials and course workbooks developed for this program are available from the Center for $35.

Center for Family Business
P.O. Box 24268
5862 Mayfield Road
Cleveland, OH 44124
216-442-0800

Members are "presidents, owner/managers, founders, and inheritors of family-owned businesses and independent, private, or closely-held companies." The Center develops educational programs for members in areas of business management, management succession, and business continuity. The Center also provides consultation and holds seminars. Publishes a monthly newsletter.

Center for Innovation and Business Development
Box 8103
University Station
Grand Forks, ND 58202
701-777-3132

The Center "provides business and technical support services to entrepreneurs, inventors, and small manufacturers in North Dakota and Northwest Minnesota." They foster "homegrown" ventures or expansion and diversification of existing companies. The Center sells the "Entrepreneur Kit", a do-it-yourself guide for people planning to start a new business. The Kit includes a Business Plan guide and a Marketing Plan guide which provide "valuable insight and will help you address the necessary issues, avoid the pitfalls, and work out some of the bugs before you get started" in your new business. Cost of the Kit is $60.

Chicago High Tech Association
20 North Wacker Drive
Suite 1929
Chicago, IL 60606
312-641-0311

Chicago High Tech Association links "together the myriad resources and informal networks available in the Chicago area to help the growth and development of technology-based ventures."

Distributive Education Clubs of America
1908 Association Drive
Reston, VA 22091
703-860-5000

The Clubs are for high school juniors and seniors and junior college students interested in marketing and distribution, both retail and wholesale.

Enterprise Publishing Co., Inc.
725 Market Street
Wilmington, DE 19801
302-654-0110

Enterprise publishes nonfiction books on business, economics, legal self-help, business how-to, and other subjects of interest to small business owners and entrepreneurs. Write for a catalog of books available.

EPIE Institute
Water Mill, NY 11976
516-621-5950

EPIE is a non-profit organization that evaluates educational computer software.

Family Computing Magazine
730 Broadway
New York, NY 10003
212-505-3580

This monthly magazine is published by Scholastic, Inc. It covers most computer topics in an easy to read and understand style. Special areas of coverage each month include children's education, home office, and a special section called K-Power, mainly topics for kids, but of interest to adults, too.

The Foundation for Entrepreneurial Excellence
Florida Southern College
111 Lake Hollingsworth Drive
Lakeland, FL 33801
813-680-4111

The Foundation provides scholarships to Florida

Southern College and DePauw University for disadvantaged minority youth. The goal of the Foundation is to "identify and assist in the development of young entrepreneurs whose dreams and visions create employment opportunities and wealth, not only for themselves, but for many others in the process."

Foundation for Student Communication
305 Aaron Burr Hall
Princeton University
Princeton, NJ 08540
609-921-1111

The Foundation promotes communication between students and businesspersons. The group produces *Business Today* magazine, the largest student-run publication in the U.S.

Foundation for Teaching Economics
555 California Street
Suite 4600
San Francisco, CA 94104
415-981-5671

The Foundation's goal is to "make economic instruction an integral part of junior high curricula." It makes available filmstrips, textbooks for students and teachers, and computer software.

Future Farmers of America
National FFA Center
Box 15160
5632 Mt. Vernon Memorial Highway
Alexandria, VA 22309
703-360-3600

The FFA offers training opportunities for public

secondary school students planning on careers in agriculture or agribusiness. The *National Future Farmer Magazine* is published bi-monthly.

Girl Scouts of the U.S.A.
830 Third Ave. and 51st St.
New York City, NY 10016
212-940-7500

The purpose of the Girl Scouts is "to help girls develop as happy, resourceful individuals willing to share their abilities as citizens in their homes, their communities, their country and the world." The organization offers leadership training and conferences and seminars on all sorts of topics from management to child development. The group, however, discourages girls from earning money other than to support troop/group activities, although the development of money management skills is encouraged for personal as well as group use.

Growing Without Schooling
Holt Associates
729 Boylston Street
Boston, MA 02116
617-437-1550

The group specializes in home schooling information.

Hewitt Research Foundation
Box 9
Washougal, WA 98671
206-835-8708

The Foundation specializes in home schooling information.

Hispanic Organization of Professionals and Executives
87 Catoctin Court
Silver Spring, MD 20906
301-598-2535

The Organization "promotes Hispanic participation in free enterprise and political systems." It encourages the formation of private enterprise endeavors and community programs.

Hugh O'Brian Youth Foundation
10880 Wilshire Blvd.
Suite 1500
Los Angeles, CA 90024
213-474-4370

The purpose of the Foundation is to "seek out, recognize, and reward leadership potential in American and international high school sophomores by sponsoring annual state and international seminars focusing on the American democratic process and economic system." The Foundation "encourages and aids young people in their struggle for self-identification and self-development."

Illinois Business Hall of Fame
Western Illinois University
Macomb, IL 61455
309-298-1594

The Hall of Fame "seeks to foster pride in the free enterprise system and in the tradition of business leadership which has made that system work so well."

International Center for Franchise Studies
The University of Nebraska - Lincoln
1237 R Street
Suite 203-0223
Lincoln, NE 68588-0223
402-472-5181

The Center hopes to eventually "become the national and international authoritative source of information pertaining to all facets of the franchise system of business."

Joint Council on Economic Education
2 Park Avenue
New York, NY 10016
212-685-5499

The Council supports economic education "by improving the quality and increasing the quantity of economics being taught in schools and colleges." The Council sponsors workshops and seminars and offers consulting services to educators.

Junior Achievement
550 Summer Street
Stamford, CT 06901
203-359-2970

Junior Achievement's main purpose is to "provide young people with practical economic education programs and experiences in the competitive private enterprise system through a partnership with the business and education communities." Maintains the National Business Hall of Fame. Offers programs in Business Basics for 5th and 6th graders, Project Business for 8th and 9th graders, and Applied Economics for 11th and 12th graders.

Kids Computer News
The Computer Club of St. Hilda's and St. Hugh's
School
619 West 114th Street
New York, NY 10025

Kids Computer News is a newsletter published by kids for kids. The newsletter provides "reviews, hints and tips, programs, computer art, humor, and articles." Subscription price is $6/year.

Manpower Administration
U.S. Department of Labor
Washington, DC 20213
202-523-6666

The Administration can provide information on nearly 350 apprenticeable trades and provide contacts in your local area.

Money Management Camp for Kids
The Breakers Hotel
Palm Beach, FL
305-655-6611

Summer money management camp for kids, 10-15 years, teaching the stock exchange, mutual funds, and other money matters. Sponsored by The Breakers and Shearson Lehman Brothers. Cost of the camp is $250 for one week program.

Nation's Business Magazine
Chamber of Commerce of the United States
1615 H St. NW
Washington, DC 20062
202-463-5650

This monthly magazine covers various business subjects as they relate to the government.

National Association for Female Executives
1041 Third Avenue, 2nd Floor
New York, NY 10021
212-371-0740
The Association's purpose is to "make women aware of the need for planning for career and financial success and to create tools to support these goals."

National Association for the Cottage Industry
P.O. Box 14460
Chicago, IL 60614
312-472-8116
The Association is for "people who work in their homes, either producing merchandise, providing services or using a flexible work site, such as a computer terminal in the home connected to a main system." Publishes a bimonthly newsletter.

National Association for the Self-Employed
2324 Gravel Road
Ft. Worth, TX 76118
817-589-2475
The Association's purpose is to promote "American small business in the free enterprise system for the self-employed, managers of small business, and owners of closely-held corporations, and to protect and promote the economic and general welfare of American small business." It offers business and tax seminars.

National Association of Black Women Entrepreneurs
P.O. Box 1375
Detroit, MI 48231
313-961-7714
The Association is made up of black women who

own and operate their own businesses and those interested in starting their own businesses. Its objective is to "enhance business, professional and technical development of both present and future black businesswomen." The Association also gives out the annual Black Woman Entrepreneur of the Year Award.

National Association of Minority Women in Business
906 Grand Avenue
Suite 500
Kansas City, MO 64116
816-421-3335

The Association is a "network for the exchange of ideas and information on business opportunities for minority women in the public and private sectors." It offers workshops, seminars, speakers bureaus, and conferences.

National Association of Women Business Owners
600 South Federal Street
Suite 400
Chicago, IL 60605
312-346-2330

The purpose of the Association is to "identify and bring together women business owners in mutual support; to communicate and share talents with others; and to use collective influence to broaden opportunities for women in business." The Association conducts workshops, seminars, an information clearinghouse, and reader and referral services. The NAWBO offers members a bimonthy newsletter, national conference, special reports, networking opportunities, management and technical assistance, and other benefits.

National Business League
4324 Georgia Avenue, NW
Washington, DC 20011
202-829-5900

The League promotes the economic development of minorities and encourages "minority ownership and management of small businesses and supports full minority participation within the free enterprise system."

National Center for Young Entrepreneurs
Suite 3200
Steinberg Hall-Dietrich Hall
Philadelphia, PA 19104-6374
215-898-9678

The NCYE is "dedicated to exposing high school students to the world of entrepreneurship by providing a wide variety of programs, opportunities, and resources."

National Federation of Independent Business
150 West 20th Avenue
San Mateo, CA 94403
415-341-7441

The Federation is made up of independent business and professional people. It gathers and releases opinions of small business to state and federal legislatures, and provides monthly press releases to high schools, colleges, and universities.

National Home Business Report
P.O. Box 2137
Department NHBR
Naperville, IL 60566

The Report is a quarterly newsletter offering tips for those interested in operating a business at home. One year subscription is $18.

National Schools Committee for Economic Education
P.O. Box 295
86 Valley Road
Cos Cob, CT 06807
203-869-1706
The Committee attempts to maintain "a continuous research and development program in ways and means, aids, and materials, to help school teachers teach the fundamental principles underlying the American economic system and the traditional values of which this system is a part."

Office for Entrepreneurial Studies
M/C 243
The University of Illinois at Chicago
Box 4348
Chicago, IL 60680
312-996-7000
The mission of the Office for Entrepreneurial Studies is "to expand awareness and knowledge among students, entrepreneurs, and professionals regarding new venture/smaller company opportunities, methods for creating and building such enterprises, and the role of entrepreneurship and new/smaller firms in economic development and the world economy."

Office of Private Sector Initiatives
Small Business Administration
1441 L Street NW
Suite 720A
Washington, DC 20416
202-653-7880
The Small Business Administration provides management education, loans, and business training information.

Online Access Guide
53 West Jackson Blvd.
Chicago, IL 60604
312-922-9292

Online Access Guide is a magazine providing information on computer databases, bulletin boards, and other materials concerning access to business information available through current online networks.

Rocky Mountain Investors Congress
P. O. Box 4365
Denver, CO 80204
303-443-3818

The RMIC is a non-profit organization which provides "a forum for investors, entrepreneurs, innovators and practical thinkers of all ages and specialties." Monthly programs and an annual conference are held to assist members in developing their own products and businesses.

Sativa
P. O. Box 2410
Station A
Champaign, IL 61820

Sativa is a cooperative exchange network that arranges work-stays on organic farms, homesteads, and gardens in the Midwest. Visitors donate their labor to growers in return for room, board, and hands-on training. No salary but you do gain experience. Time of visit is up to individual, ranging from a weekend to several months.

Service Corps of Retired Executives Association
1129 20th Street, NW
Suite 410
Washington, DC 20416
202-653-6279

SCORE is a volunteer organization made up of active and retired businesspeople who provide free assistance to people interested in starting a small business, expanding their business, or needing advice in their present business.

State of New York
Banking Department
Two Rector Street
New York, NY 10006
212-618-6642

The Banking Department — in cooperation with Cornell University, the NY State Education Department, and the NY State Council on Economic Education — has produced a videotape program entitled "You're Accountable." The program "deals with financial problems facing young adults and covers such banking topics as selecting the proper savings vehicle to meet particular goals, the selection and utilization of a checking account and the importance of comparison shopping when seeking a loan." This tape is being distributed to 1,500 high schools across New York state.

Success Magazine
342 Madison Avenue
New York, NY 10173
212-916-3400

Founded by W. Clement Stone, *Success* magazine offers readers "new strategies, techniques and opportunities for moving ahead, moving up (and making more money)."

Successful American Entrepreneurs Magazine
3918 Sandlewood
Pasadena, TX 77504
713-373-3535

This magazine is published by the Kwik-Kopy Corporation. It prints stories of "Americans who have taken risks and have ultimately succeeded...the ones who embody the free enterprise system." Subscription price is $5 per year for the quarterly magazine.

United States Association for Small Business and
Entrepreneurship
Institute for Business
Chicopee Building
University of Georgia
Athens, GA 30602
404-542-5760

The USASBE includes professionals in education, industry, finance, and government. Through publications, networking, and special conferences, the USASBE provides "the opportunity for business professionals to interact and exchange innovative ideas and methods...successes and failures."

Vocational Industrial Clubs of America
P.O. Box 3000
Leesburg, VA 22075
703-777-8810

The Clubs are for students in trade, industrial, technical, and health occupations programs in schools. The group sponsors the VICA U. S. Skill Olympics and provides lectures and programs for school and community groups.

Women Entrepreneurs
2030 Union Street
Suite 310
San Francisco, CA 94123
415-929-0129

This group offers support, recognition, and access to information and resources to women who actively own or operate a business. They also conduct monthly workshops and seminars.

Young Entrepreneur's Hotline
P.O. Box 208
Williston, ND 58802

The Hotline is a newsletter designed to "provide stories about successful young business people and how they are helping other young people. It is also to provide solid, factual information for the many questions aspiring entrepreneurs have so they can put it to work right away." One year subscription is $24.

Young Investors Association
8116 Langdon Street
Philadelphia, PA 19152
215-342-5333

The YIA's goal is "to set up a network of young people interested in the markets so that they can exchange ideas and information on particular stocks and other investments."

Young President's Organization
52 Vanderbilt Avenue
New York, NY 10017
212-867-1900

Members are elected corporate presidents between the ages of 40 and 50. Conducts business seminars on a variety of topics.

INDEX